Best of
Boulder Climbs

Jeff Lowe on Left Wing, Third Elephant Buttress, Boulder Canyon

Best of Boulder Climbs

Richard Rossiter

Chockstone Press
Evergreen, Colorado

ISBN 0-934641-26-9

PUBLISHED AND DISTRIBUTED BY
Chockstone Press, Inc.
Post Office Box 3505
Evergreen, CO 80439

Front: Gary Ryan on Sunrider, Eldorado Canyon. Photo by Beth Wald.
Back: Joyce Rossiter on College Dropout, Third Flatiron. Photo by author.

All uncredited photos are by the author.

Guaranteed Binding
This book binding is sewn with nylon thread to withstand the rough treatment of the active climber. OUR GUARANTEE: If the binding of this book falls apart send us the book and we will replace it with a good copy of the same edition.

Preface

BEST OF BOULDER CLIMBS IS A SYNOPSIS OF THE more comprehensive guide books, *Boulder Climbs North* and *Boulder Climbs South*. It contains a selection of the best climbs from both books, plus a good number of superior routes not previously published. The production of such a book incurs the onerous task of deciding which routes to include and which to leave out. From this consideration, a survey of suggested routes was sent out to more than 50 of the area's most experienced climbers for approval and revision. I targeted not only the gnarliest of the hardmen but also veteran weekend warriors and Flatiron slab mongers. The survey allowed participants to add to the list, accept it as it was, make deletions and change ratings of difficulty. This approach not only gives the book undeniable authority beyond my personal opinion, it also diffuses the inevitable grumbling about selections among all who participated in the survey.

As the results were tallied, I found that a large number of the routes selected were ones completed in the last three years, which indicates a very strong leaning toward bolt-protected face climbing. Naturally, timeless classics such as the Naked Edge, the Yellow Spur and the Bastille Crack were not overlooked. In fact, routes such as these got the highest ratings. The highest score for any route was 32 votes (the Yellow Spur); the lowest was a minus 2. The easiest and the hardest routes had relatively lower scores than the mid-range, simply because fewer people climb at either extreme. Routes that received 10 or more votes are featured in this book as the *Best of Boulder*. Other good routes within reasonable proximity to these are sometimes described. Occasionally, routes shown in the topos do not appear in the text; this is done simply for clarification in identifying featured routes. The results also indicated that the book should feature crags with groupings of good routes and avoid relatively isolated climbs, which, for the most part, is what I have done. I hereby take refuge in the role of editor and present to the reader a consensus with clout – and a distinguished list of scapegoats.

ACKNOWLEDGMENTS

I would like to thank the following people for completing surveys and making this guide book a more interesting project: Pat Adams, Fran Bagenal, Allen Bartlett, Phillip Benningfield, Bobbi Bensman, Roger Briggs, Rob Candelaria, Chip Chase, Monica Chase, Steve Conolly, the Crusher, Bill DeMallie, Mike Downing, Gene Ellis, Mic Fairchild, Mike Gilbert, Christian Griffith, Dan Hare, Bob Horan, Derek Hersey, Steve Ilg, Christy Jesperson, Alan Jolley, Randy Josephs, Marty Kim, Colin Lantz, Jim Michaels, Steve Muehlhauser, Gary Neptune, Charlie Oliver, Paul Piana, Mark Rolofson, Steve Ross, Joyce Rossiter, Chip Ruckgaber, Bret Ruckman, Wolfgang Schweiger, Sarah Spalding, Johnna Tipton, Ed Webster, Austin Weiss and Rob Woolf.

Gerry Roach gave permission to average into the survey results the "classic" and "top ten" routes from his fine pocket guide, *Flatiron Classics*. A special thank you goes to Gene Ellis for proofreading and to Pat Ament for sending a list of his favorite routes.

Derek Hersey on Land of Ra, Cadillac Crag

Contents ────────────────────────

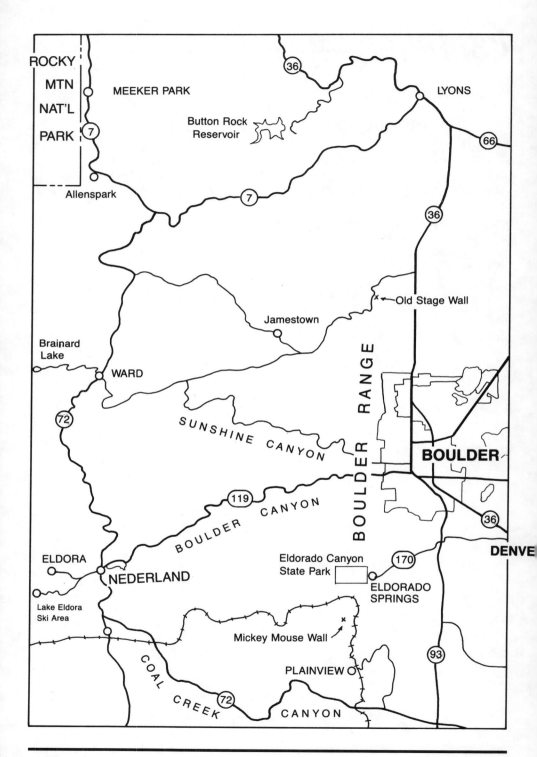

Introduction ————————————————————

BOULDER, COLORADO HAS LONG BEEN RECOGNIZED as one of the world's great climbing centers. Its tremendous concentration of crags, short approaches and proximity to Rocky Mountain National Park have made Boulder a port of call for climbers from around the globe. The Flatirons and Eldorado Canyon offer excellent routes up to eight pitches long on very hard, conglomerate sandstone, while Boulder Canyon presents a good variety of crack and face climbs on clean granite. A wide selection of routes at every level of difficulty can be found throughout the area. The vast local climbing population has always been friendly to visiting climbers and one can expect a lot of sunny weather from spring to late autumn.

As in other popular and well-developed climbing areas, there has been a certain amount of political upheaval within and about the sport that at times has taken some of the fun out of it. The violent and largely unnecessary schism regarding the use of fixed protection erupted in Boulder with as much furor as anywhere in the United States. Partly, if not primarily, as a result of this ludicrous debacle, two local land management areas have cracked down on bolting and may limit climber access with Boulder Mountain Parks leading the way in restrictive policy. Specifically, bolting of new routes currently is illegal in both Eldorado and the Flatirons. Fortunately, the removal of fixed protection also is illegal, which means existing routes are now protected by law. The Eldorado management plan will allow for limited new routes and maintenance of existing fixed gear, the latter of which is just common sense. The Boulder Mountain Parks plan makes no such allowances.

Fortunately, the basic freedoms and pleasures of rock climbing are still here to be enjoyed. The company of a friend, the love of the wild places, artistry, adventure, unification of self and world, all are part of the essential nature of an activity that is too grand to be dominated by the mannerisms of a particular generation or the mercurial policies of government agencies. Thus, there is the larger, invisible aspect of rock climbing that is experiential and has always been available to those who venture onto the rocky heights.

Camping

None of the areas covered in this guide offer camping, nor is camping available in adjacent areas close enough to be of use to visiting climbers. The only exception is a KOA campground on East Valmont Road (northeast Boulder). Otherwise, one must drive to Golden Gate Canyon State Park, Rocky Mountain National Park, or the Indian Peaks Wilderness to find legal camping. The nearest of these areas to Eldorado Canyon is Golden Gate Canyon State Park, which is one-hour's drive distant. All Front Range campgrounds may reach capacity even on weeknights during the summer, and of course, they are closed during the snowy winters. Commercial lodging such as motels and hotels are many, but may not be of interest to traveling climbers. Welcome to Boulder.

An alternative is the Boulder International Youth Hostel, located at 1107 12th Street, Boulder, Colorado 80302. Telephone: (303) 442-0522. Daily rates are $6 for members, $8 for nonmembers. The Nederland Youth Hostel is at 1005 Jackson Street, Nederland, Colorado 80466. Telephone: (303) 258-9925. Daily rate: $4.50. The Boulder KOA campground is at 5856 Valmont Road, Boulder, Colorado 80301 and is $9 per site.

Weather

People who are relatively new to this area – excepting southern Californians – seem never to cease commenting upon the mild winters and pleasant summers. Even some long-term residents hold this opinion, and we must suppose that compared to the Midwest or the Atlantic Seaboard, the contrast would support such a view. Others, especially rock climbers, may find Boulder valley weather somewhat annoying; but it is true that living in Boulder, one may become fussy and spoiled.

In the winter, there usually is a pronounced period of balmy, sunny weather that comes between the first heavy snows (with lows near zero) and the unsettled and frequently snowy weather of late winter and spring. These days of winter sun may occur at any time from late December to mid-March. Other sunny days, especially in the fall, feature gale-force winds that may reach 100 miles per hour. "Spring" is in quotation marks because it usually snows long after the flowers and leaves have come out and most Boulderites have left for vacations in Mexico and Hawaii. The warm, clear weather that one ordinarily associates with summer lies between June and September, but frequently is punctuated by violent thunderstorms with heavy precipitation (hail and/or rain). By October, the weather cools noticeably and the first snows may be expected. There usually is a brief respite of clear autumm weather into early November, followed by heavy snows and the onset of winter.

On Equipment

A few practical considerations on equipment may be of service to those new to the area or new to a particular route. In the event of wide cracks, sustained thin cracks, or other unusual situations, additional equipment suggestions are included with the route desriptions. Otherwise, the following gear is recommended:

A set of RPs
Other wired stoppers up to one inch
2 or 3 slung stoppers
2 or 3 Hexs or Tri-cams
Various camming devices up to two inches (#3 Friend)
7 or 8 quickdraws (QD)
5 or 6 runners long enough to wear over the shoulder
6 to 8 unoccupied carabiners (usually with the runners)

Important: If equipment suggestions are not included in a route description, it implies that the gear listed above is recommended.

Ratings

The system used in this book for rating difficulty is a descendant of the so-called Yosemite Decimal System, which, in turn, is a descendant of a system developed at Tahquitz Rock and introduced by the Sierra Club in 1937. This was based on the German Welzenbach grades, which divided terrain difficulty into six classes according to the techniques and equipment one would typically employ. Class one, for example, was merely steep, off-trail hiking. Class three was harder, requiring the frequent use of hands and basic free-climbing techniques. Class five was roped free climbing, and class six was direct aid.

By the 1950s, rock climbing had evolved to the point where six classes of difficulty from walking uphill to direct aid were a bit too broad, especially since the major focus was on class five climbing. Thus, class five was subdivided into 10 units and written as 5.0

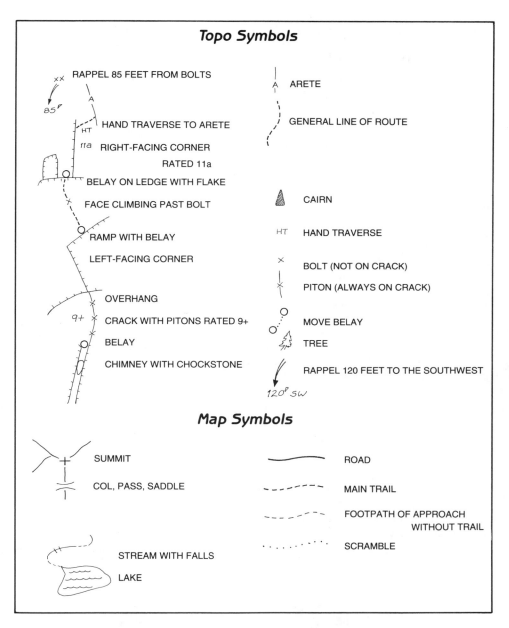

Topo Symbols

RAPPEL 85 FEET FROM BOLTS

ARETE

HAND TRAVERSE TO ARETE

GENERAL LINE OF ROUTE

RIGHT-FACING CORNER
RATED 11a

BELAY ON LEDGE WITH FLAKE

CAIRN

FACE CLIMBING PAST BOLT

RAMP WITH BELAY

HAND TRAVERSE

LEFT-FACING CORNER

BOLT (NOT ON CRACK)

PITON (ALWAYS ON CRACK)

OVERHANG

CRACK WITH PITONS RATED 9+

MOVE BELAY

BELAY

TREE

CHIMNEY WITH CHOCKSTONE

RAPPEL 120 FEET TO THE SOUTHWEST

Map Symbols

SUMMIT

ROAD

COL, PASS, SADDLE

MAIN TRAIL

FOOTPATH OF APPROACH
WITHOUT TRAIL

SCRAMBLE

STREAM WITH FALLS

LAKE

through 5.9, while class six was divided into five units and written as A1 through A5. This worked well enough until a climb was completed that was harder than 5.9, which necessitated the numerical absurdity of 5.10 or the development of a new rating system. As we all know, American climbers settled for the former.

By the early 1970s, free climbing was sufficiently well-developed in Yosemite that the subdivisions a, b, c and d were added to grades 5.10 and harder, further complicating an illogical system that, by comparison, makes inches, feet and yards look rather well thought out. Though most of us are used to it, the "decimal system" is a dinosaur looking for a place to die, and I would like to give it an opportunity to do so with this book.

If we eliminate the original six classes of the Welzenbach system and drop the decimal point, we are left with an open-ended series of whole numbers from 0 to 14 (onward if needed) that represents all levels of roped free climbing and does not require reassignment of ratings to existing routes. 5.4 simply becomes 4, 5.9+ becomes 9+, and 5.12c becomes 12c. The letter grades a, b, c and d, and perhaps the +, are useful and can be applied as before. As for easier terrain, it is enough to know that it is a walk or a scramble and need not be further subdivided into numerical categories. Thus, we have a logical, streamlined system, the application of which requires very little adjustment and is easily comprehended by the uninitiated.

In 1980, Jim Erickson introduced a simple system for rating the seriousness of a climb in terms of available protection. In his popular pocket guide, *Rocky Heights,* he uses the ratings PG, R, and X, which he borrowed from the American movie industry. I have not employed these particular ratings in my books because I viewed them as a product of Jim's whimsical sense of humor, and I did not want to plagiarize his idea. They have, however, come into wide application in other guide books, making me the odd man out for not using them.

In this book, as well as other guides that I have produced, the potential for a long leader fall is indicated by an s (serious) or vs (very serious) after the rating of difficulty. A climb rated s will have at least one notable runout and the potential for a scary fall. A climb rated vs typically will have poor protection for hard moves and the potential for a fatal or near-fatal fall. The absence of these letters indicates a relatively safe climb, provided it is within the leader's ability.

At best, all ratings assigned to climbs represent the concensus of climbers, that is to say, opinion and nothing more. It is essential to remember that this is only a guide to the routes; in the end, it is your skill and judgement that will keep you alive on the rocks.

Environmental Considerations

Appreciation for the frailty and scarcity of wilderness is more universal today than it has ever been. Yet climbers, who might stand at the vanguard of such vision, are lagging behind. There is a tendency to become so focused on our projects and accomplishments that we lose our environmental perspective. Thus, we may plow up and down talus fields like mindless drunkards, trample wildflowers, and leave adhesive tape, chalk wrappers, nylon slings, toilet paper and other debris in the places where we climb. This lugubrious state of affairs clearly is not exacerbated by all climbers, but by enough that the impact is visible and omnipresent.

Our approach to climbing is a reflection of our approach to life, and we have a long way to go to master the art of living on this planet. While the world population swells to astronomical proportions, we have developed powerful technologies capable of drastically upsetting – or utterly destroying – the balance of planetary life. This is not happening by accident, and it is not out of control. To the contrary, the sad state of our world is the direct and continuing result of the choices we make each day. It is my feeling that mankind has complete dominion over his destiny through the expression of his will, and sadly, we have willed much that is destructive, violent and biologically untenable, which continues to degrade life with enormous momentum. A degree of this brashness has been brought into the sport of climbing.

What each one of us does makes a difference. A few suggestions are offered. Deposit solid human waste far from the cliffs and away from paths of approach and descent. Do not cover with a rock, but leave it exposed to the elements where it will deteriorate more quickly. Carry used toilet paper out in a plastic bag or use a stick or Douglas fir cone. Do not leave man-made riff-raff lying about. If you pack it in, pack it out. Use chalk sparingly. Do not leave slings hanging from bolts or pins. Since dangling slings have become a point of contention with park managers, it would be better to move bolts to where they can be reached than to leave "cheater slings" hanging on them. Take care to preserve trees and other plants on approaches and climbs. Scree gullies and talus fields ususally have sections that are more stable – thrashing up and down loose scree causes erosion and destroys flora. Always use trails and footpaths where they have been developed, and demonstrate human evolution by removing obstructions, stacking loose rocks along the trail sides and picking up trash. Respect area closures for nesting raptors.

So much fuss has been made about fixed protection – yet, from an environmental point of view, the use of pitons and bolts is, by any stretch of the imagination, utterly insignificant. The entire sport of climbing has no bearing at all on whether life survives on this planet, or even on the quality of life. Whether one sanctions or disdains the use of bolts must, in all fairness, be viewed as a matter of taste. If climbing has a real and measurable environmental impact, it is in soil erosion and loss of plants from foot traffic to and from routes. This problem, which dates back half a century, is due largely to the carelessness of climbers and to the fact that the parks have been very slow in responding to the need for approach trails.

Fixed protection has always been a part of climbing and it will no doubt continue to be. It simply provides access to the rock. Some park officals have taken the position that bolts and pitons should be illegal because they "deface" natural features. But by that reasoning, they should have to remove all trails, roads, signs, parking lots, souvenir shops, restaurants and ranger stations, any of which have done thousands of times more to deface natural features than all of the bolts and pins ever placed. I am certainly not suggesting that every possible route be bolted. It is just that the sport of climbing could not exist in most areas without fixed protection; there would not be enough routes of reasonable safety and quality to keep people interested. The recently lauded and so-called "clean climbing" era of the 1970s was made possible by the fact that a great deal of fixed protection had been placed during the "aid climbing" era of the 1960s. Most of the routes featured in this book – old and new – simply would not exist without fixed protection.

The old and excruciatingly boring debate over whether fixed protection should be placed on the lead or from a top rope is so much swamp sludge. If you like ground-up ethics, then work from the ground up. If you like to hang-dog, then hang. If you like to free-solo, nobody's stopping you. The whole issue is silly. If you want to get shook up, try pro wrestling or national politics. If you want to save the environment, harping on bolts won't make any difference at all. Instead, sell your car and buy a bicycle. The important thing is to get out there and enjoy yourself. A day is a terrible thing to waste, and who knows how many more you've got. Climb as it pleases you, leave others to do the same and save the rhetoric. Personally, I'd rather just go climbing.

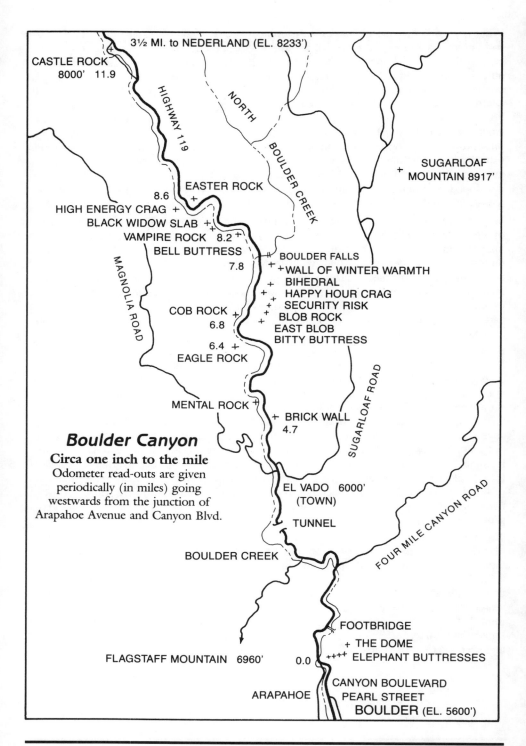

3½ MI. to NEDERLAND (EL. 8233')

CASTLE ROCK
8000' 11.9

HIGHWAY 119

NORTH BOULDER CREEK

SUGARLOAF
MOUNTAIN 8917'

EASTER ROCK

8.6
HIGH ENERGY CRAG +
BLACK WIDOW SLAB +
VAMPIRE ROCK 8.2 +
BELL BUTTRESS

7.8

MAGNOLIA ROAD

BOULDER FALLS
+ WALL OF WINTER WARMTH
+ BIHEDRAL
+ HAPPY HOUR CRAG
+ SECURITY RISK
+ BLOB ROCK
EAST BLOB
BITTY BUTTRESS

COB ROCK +
6.8

6.4 +
EAGLE ROCK

SUGARLOAF ROAD

MENTAL ROCK +

+ BRICK WALL
4.7

Boulder Canyon
Circa one inch to the mile
Odometer read-outs are given
periodically (in miles) going
westwards from the junction of
Arapahoe Avenue and Canyon Blvd.

EL VADO 6000'
(TOWN)

TUNNEL

FOUR MILE CANYON ROAD

BOULDER CREEK

FLAGSTAFF MOUNTAIN 6960'   0.0

FOOTBRIDGE
+ THE DOME
++++ ELEPHANT BUTTRESSES

CANYON BOULEVARD
PEARL STREET
BOULDER (EL. 5600')

ARAPAHOE

Boulder Canyon

BOULDER CANYON'S GREAT ASSORTMENT of granite domes and buttresses offers a pleasant alternative to the sandstone crags of Eldorado and the Flatirons. The canyon is about 16 miles long and climbs west – nearly from downtown Boulder – to the mountain town of Nederland. There are many high-quality routes from one to three pitches, typically not far from the road. The sun-drenched, south-facing crags on the north side of the canyon offer luxurious accommodations when it is too cold to climb elsewhere.

Springtime brings high water to Boulder Creek, which makes fords to the south side of the canyon difficult or impossible. Another feature of spring – or should I say, creature of spring – is the wood tick. Abundant and persistent, these little invaders carry a virus that causes tick fever. But they move slowly; pick them off before they become imbedded in the skin. By mid to late summer, the water level recedes, affording access to all southside crags. However, one should bear in mind that the stream flow is subject to human manipulation and may, during any season, increase or decrease unexpectedly.

Boulder Canyon is reached easily from downtown Boulder by going west on Canyon Boulevard (Highway 119), which travels the length of the canyon to Nederland. A short way west of Boulder city limits, the highway crosses Boulder Creek on a bridge from which mileages to the various crags are measured.

For those interested in winter ice climbing, Boulder Falls (about 7.5 miles) freezes when it has been very cold and offers a short pitch of blue ice. Of greater interest are several rivulets of ice formed by an aqueduct leak, just west of Castle Rock (about 11.5 miles) and on the south side of the road.

ELEPHANT BUTTRESSES

About one-half mile up the highway and on the north stand four bulky towers, which are numbered one through four, north to south. One easily may walk or ride a bicycle to these popular formations via the Boulder Creek Path. To approach by car, drive past the formations to an obvious pull-out on the right. Park here, then walk north across a steel bridge. Turn right and follow the stream bank until a path leads up onto a large, steel waterpipe. Follow the pipe to the south until directly below the buttresses. To descend from the top of any route, scramble off the east side and traverse north to the slope between The Dome and the First Elephant Buttress, then hike back down to the steel pipe. Or very carefully downclimb the gully between the Second and Third Buttresses (4). The First Elephant Buttress is not described in this book.

SECOND ELEPHANT BUTTRESS
1. **Avalon Rising   12b/c**
   Follow a line of bolts up the arete to the left of Classic Finger Crack. 4 QD, #6 Rock.
2. **Classic Finger Crack   9**
   Belay at the top of an easy gully, then climb an aesthetic, thin crack in the steep face. 50 feet.

THIRD ELEPHANT BUTTRESS

1. **Wingtip   10c**
   This fine, short climb takes the steep, left-facing dihedral up and left from Left Wing. Begin about 70 feet up the descent gully.

2. **Left Wing   10c**
   Scramble about 60 feet up the descent gully and move out right to a ledge. Climb the obvious left-leaning, left-facing dihedral.

3. **What's Up?   10d**
   Climb the first 40 feet of Left Wing, then lieback around a square roof on the right.

4. **FM   11c**
   Stupendous. Begin a short way up the descent gully from the pipe and climb up into an A-shaped roof. Move left, then straight up into the fray. Bring extra RPs.

5. **Standard Route   7 or 9**
   Begin climbing from the water pipe a short way right of the descent gully.

6. **Monster Woman   8+**
   Begin at a slab with a large eyebolt just right of the Standard Route, and power up through the roof. Join the Standard Route.

FOURTH ELEPHANT BUTTRESS

1. **Zolar Czakl   10a s**
   Begin with a flake (10a) that is almost in the cave between the Third and Fourth Buttresses, or with a left-angling crack around to the right (9).

2. **Northwest Face   8**
   Traverse out to the right for about 25 or 30 feet from where the pipe enters the cave, then up and slightly left in a crack system.

SECOND ELEPHANT BUTTRESS
2. Classic Finger Crack 9
THIRD ELEPHANT BUTTRESS
2. Left Wing 10c
5. Standard Route 7 or 9
FOURTH ELEPHANT BUTTRESS
2. Northwest Face 8

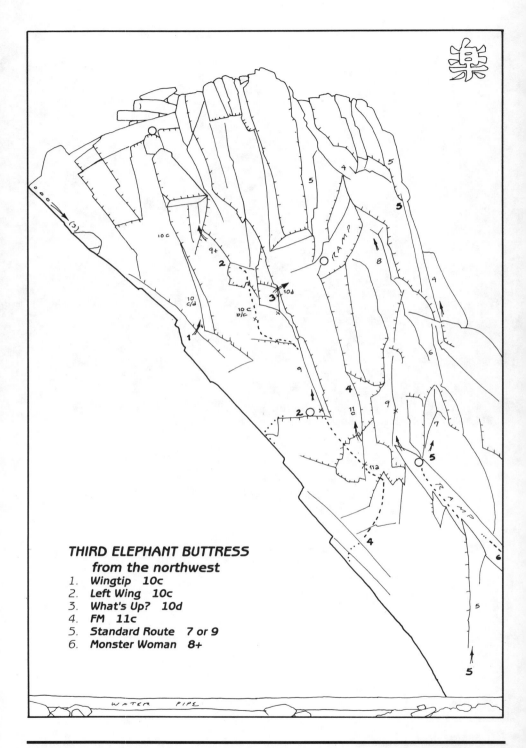

THIRD ELEPHANT BUTTRESS
from the northwest
1. Wingtip   10c
2. Left Wing   10c
3. What's Up?   10d
4. FM   11c
5. Standard Route   7 or 9
6. Monster Woman   8+

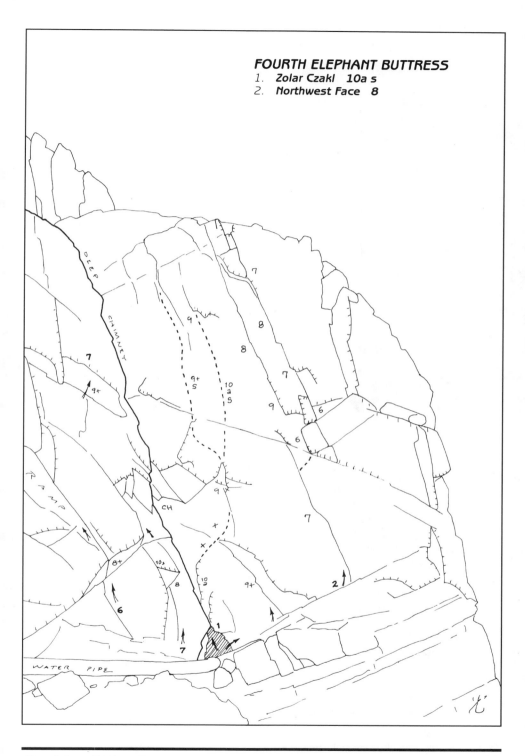

FOURTH ELEPHANT BUTTRESS
1. Zolar Czakl   10a s
2. Northwest Face   8

THE DOME

With a warm southern exposure and good assortment of moderate routes, The Dome was destined for stardom. It lies just northwest of the First Elephant Buttress and is seen easily from the road. Approach as for the Elephant Buttresses. Descend from the top by downclimbing to the east or west.

1. **Prelude To King Kong 9**
   Begin about halfway up a large ramp, just left of a black streak.
2. **Gorilla's Delight 9**
   From the belay at the top of Prelude, climb up into the steep left-facing corner.
3. **Owl 7**
   Climb left up an easy ramp from the low point of the face, up into a short left-facing dihedral, around to the right, and up a handcrack (7) to a big ledge. Choose from several finishes.
4. **Cozyhang 7**
   Begin about 80 feet up and right of the low point of the face. Climb squiggly cracks up to three small roofs, and continue on more of the same. Three pitches.
5. **The East Slab 5**
   This probably is the finest route of its grade in the Boulder area. Begin about 120 feet up and right from the low point of the face at a short, steep dihedral.

Nancy Prichard jams the Owl, The Dome

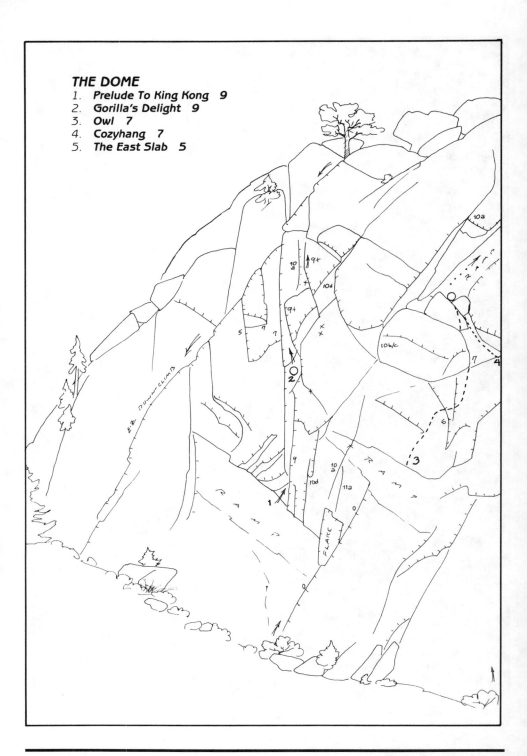

THE DOME
1. **Prelude To King Kong 9**
2. **Gorilla's Delight 9**
3. **Owl 7**
4. **Cozyhang 7**
5. **The East Slab 5**

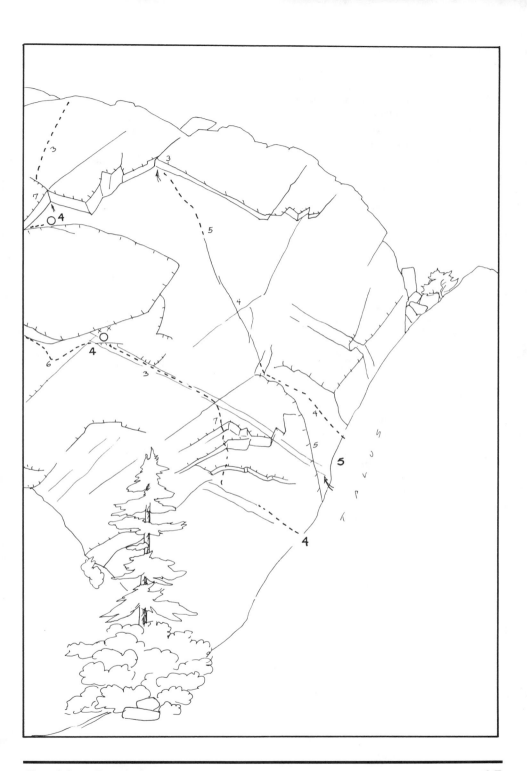

COB ROCK

At about 6.6 miles, a clean, compact buttress comes into view on the south side of the canyon. A convenient gravel turn-out exists directly in front of it. In the autumn and winter, Cob is a cold and shady place, and one may wonder why people are climbing there in duvets and Dachsteins. But perhaps this attests to the quality and great popularity of its routes. The easiest descent from the top is to scramble off to the south, then down through the trees along the west side.

At the bottom center of the north face is a 50-foot-high block with popular routes that may be led or toproped.

1. **Night Vision   10b**
   Begin just left of Huston Crack. The first bolt can be clipped from a tree. Three pitches.

2. **Huston Crack   8**
   The obvious wide crack.

3. **East Crack   10b**
   Begin as for the second pitch of Night Vision, or take the original start up a shallow left-facing corner on the right, then follow a thin crack up the beautiful face.

4. **North Face Left   8 ***
   Good crack and face climbing. Begin at the bottom of the face in a small alcove up and right from the Huston Crack block.

5. **North Face Center   7**
   Begin as for North Face Left, but after about 50 feet move into a crack system on the right.

6. **Empor   7**
   Begin at the bottom right side of the north face from the top of a large boulder. Climb a right-facing dihedral and finish with a steep jam crack.

7. **Northwest Corner   7**
   Begin as for Empor, or climb a difficult finger crack around on the right (10a). Work up the right edge of the north face to the top. Two pitches.

8. **West Rib   7**
   Farther up along the west side, climb a crack up a rock rib to join the Northwest Corner route at the overhang. Rack up to a #4 Friend.

Jeff Lowe on East Crack

COB ROCK
2. **Huston Crack   8**
3. **East Crack   10b**
4. **North Face Left   8**
5. **North Face Center   7**

6. **Empor   7**
7. **Northwest Corner   7**
8. **West Rib   7**

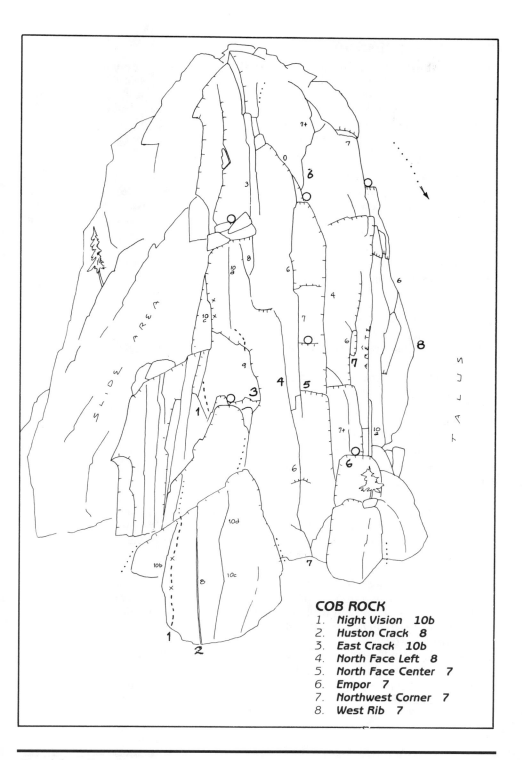

COB ROCK

1. Night Vision   10b
2. Huston Crack   8
3. East Crack   10b
4. North Face Left   8
5. North Face Center   7
6. Empor   7
7. Northwest Corner   7
8. West Rib   7

BLOB ROCK MASSIF

On the north side of the canyon directly across from Cob Rock are three large, south-facing buttresses: Blob Rock, East Blob and Bitty Buttresss, west to east. The most practical and pleasant approach is from the small parking area on the north, about 100 yards west of the Cob Rock pullout. Follow a footpath northeast past a retaining wall, then more directly up the slope to the bottom of Blob Rock. East Blob and the popular Blob Slab (the lower apron) are just to the right (east). Bitty Buttress is not described.

BLOB ROCK

A less-than-dignified name for a commanding buttress that is host to eagles and a bevy of fine routes. The approach requires a 15-minute hike up the hillside, mostly on a path. Descend by scrambling west along a broad, grassy ledge all the way to the west end of the rock. Beware of a couple of exposed traverses and a short downclimb at the end. Routes are listed from west to east across the south face.

1. **Divine Wind   11a s**
   Kamikaze in Japanese. Begin just below the right edge of a low, square roof at the far west side of the face, and follow a dihedral system for two pitches. Bring extra RPs. One can avoid the unprotected roof of the second pitch by climbing up a crack/slot just to the right (10a).

2. **Wounded Knee   11b**
   Begin with Divine Wind or an easier line to the right. Undercling and jam a stepped dihedral/roof system and finish with a slot through a large roof. Rack up to a #4 Friend.

3. **Bearcat Goes to Hollywood   11d**
   Climb the smooth face and quartz dike out to the right from Wounded Knee. Rappel or climb the roof.

4. **Eye of the Storm   10c s**
   Begin with the original start to Wounded Knee, then work up and right across the face to join Silent Running.

The following routes begin from the Central Chimney, a brushy gully that cuts diagonally up and right through the middle of the south face.

5. **The Radlands   12b**
   Perfect rock and good protection. Scramble up the Central Chimney to a ledge beneath a spike of rock and belay (#3 Friend). Work up and left across the face to a two-bolt anchor (optional belay), then up a seam to the top of the face. Rack up to a 0.5 Friend with 6 QD; 11 QD for single pitch.

6. **Silent Running   11a vs**
   This is the best moderately-difficult face climb in Boulder Canyon, but the lack of protection has kept it from becoming popular. Begin about 50 feet up the Central Gully at a 12-foot spike of rock. Stem off the spike, move up over a bulge, then work up and left along grooves and flakes.

7. **Kamikaze   10c**
   Divine Wind in English. Begin as for Silent Running, but crank right above the bulge. Follow a system of protectable grooves up and left.

8. **Gathering Storm   10c s**
   Begin at the spike as for the preceding routes, but continue up and right into a shallow, left-facing corner.

9. **The Tempest   10c**
A turbulent piano sonata by Beethoven. Begin as for the preceding routes but continue up a ramp to the right.

10. **Where Eagles Dare   10a**
Three good pitches of crack and face climbing. Begin at a big boulder about 100 feet up and right of the low point of the face.

11. **Decade Dance   10d**
From the big boulder mentioned above, continue up the gully until it is possible to scramble left onto a ledge. Climb an overhanging chimney (9+) and belay beneath the left of two cracks. Climb the hand crack on the left for about 35 feet, then traverse to the crack on the right. Rack up to a #4 Friend.

12. **Aging Time   11b**
Begin as for Decade Dance and climb the very steep crack on the right. Belay on the grassy walk-off ledge. Rack up to a #4 Friend.

EAST BLOB

This is the large, irregular formation between Blob Rock and Bitty Buttress. The following routes lie on Blob Slab, a splendid granite apron at the foot of the crag. These routes can be led or toproped from a ledge at the top of the slab.

1. **A Hike with Ludwig Dude   9 s**
Begin this 100-foot pitch near the middle of the slab, just right of a tree. Rack up to a #1 Friend.

2. **Out of Limits   10a vs**
This route usually is toproped. Begin a few feet to the right of Ludwig Dude.

3. **Crack Tack   9 s**
Begin a few feet to the right of Out of Limits. Climb straight up past a bolt, then up and slightly left to the top of the slab. One also may start by angling in from a crack on the right. Rack up to a #1 Friend.

Boulder Canyon   **21**

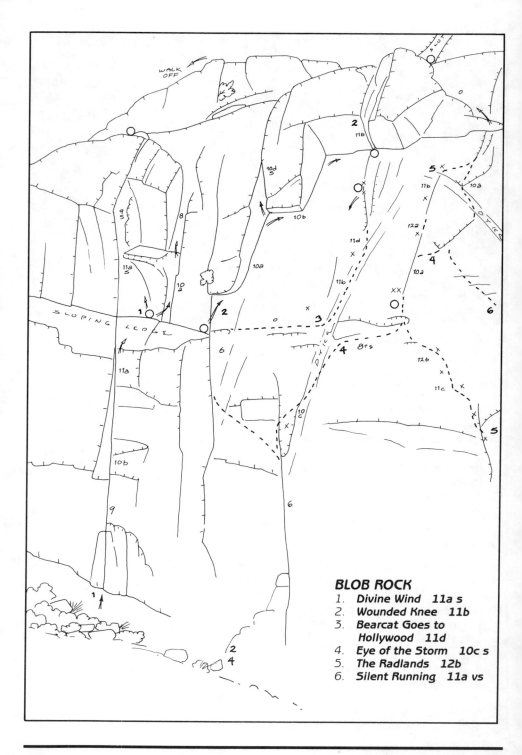

BLOB ROCK
1. Divine Wind   11a s
2. Wounded Knee   11b
3. Bearcat Goes to
   Hollywood   11d
4. Eye of the Storm   10c s
5. The Radlands   12b
6. Silent Running   11a vs

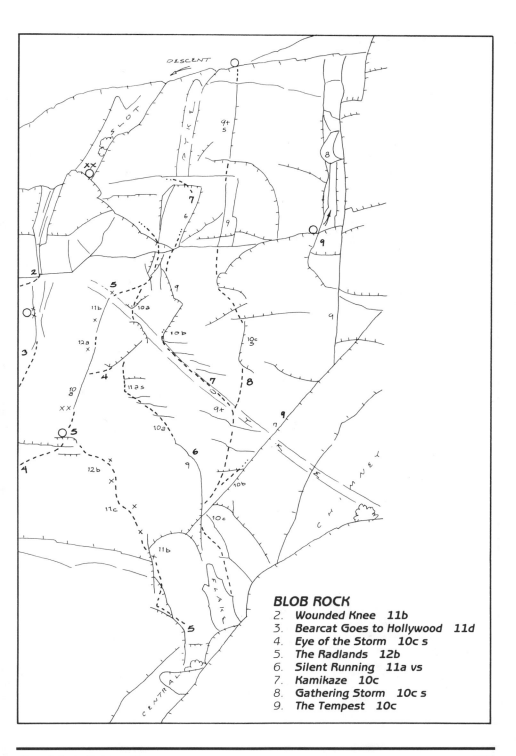

BLOB ROCK
2. *Wounded Knee* **11b**
3. *Bearcat Goes to Hollywood* **11d**
4. *Eye of the Storm* **10c s**
5. *The Radlands* **12b**
6. *Silent Running* **11a vs**
7. *Kamikaze* **10c**
8. *Gathering Storm* **10c s**
9. *The Tempest* **10c**

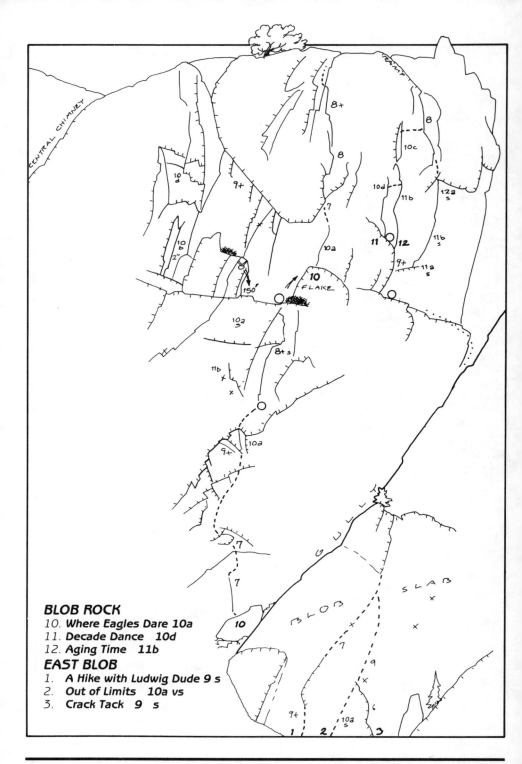

BLOB ROCK
10. *Where Eagles Dare 10a*
11. *Decade Dance   10d*
12. *Aging Time   11b*
EAST BLOB
1. *A Hike with Ludwig Dude 9 s*
2. *Out of Limits   10a vs*
3. *Crack Tack   9   s*

Joyce Rossiter on the Radlands, Blob Rock

CASTLE ROCK

Castle Rock is one of the most famous crags in Boulder Canyon. The fact that one can drive nearly to the base of every route has not hindered its popularity. The crag appears as a large, beehive-shaped formation on the south side of the road at the 12-mile mark. To descend from the summit, downclimb the North Face route or rappel from anchors at the tops of some routes.

1. **North Face 0**
   This is the easiest route to and from the summit. To descend, scramble to the north side of the summit area, then follow your nose down ramps, ledges and short cracks to the north, then west.

2. **Skunk Crack 9+**
   This route takes the left of two cracks on the nose of a small, west-facing buttress.

3. **Comeback Crack 10b/c**
   Hands and fingers just right of Skunk Crack.

4. **Curving Crack 9**
   At the right of the buttress, a nice crack curves up and left.

5. **Final Exam 11a**
   Sort of a classic. Begin a few yards to the right of a large dihedral. Pass/Fail Option (11a) takes the roof about 75 feet up.

6. **Cussin' Crack 7**
   An old standard. Begin as for Jackson's Wall, but after about 60 feet, make a long traverse up to the left. Climb straight up a distinct, V-shaped corner (crux). Three or four pitches.

7. **Western Pleasure 11a**
   Begin about 100 feet up into the trough of Jackson's Wall at a shallow dihedral with a couple of pins. Two pitches.

8. **Jackson's Wall 6**
   This is a very old and popular route, but most of the climbing is not very aesthetic. Begin in a deep cleft at the left side of a giant block. Climb a long trough and a short face (crux).

9. **Tongo 11a s**
   Climb a right-angling ramp and left-angling crack a few yards to the right of Jackson's Wall.

10. **Gill Crack 12a**
    To the right of a fire scar and a blackened crack is a thin knuckle-wrecker that will test your pain threshold. Downclimb the crack on the left, or continue upward.

11. **South Face 9**
    Also known as Jackson's Wall Direct, this is one of the best moderate routes in Boulder Canyon. Begin beneath a short, right- facing dihedral that is about midway between the fire scar and the bridge beneath Country Club Crack. Three pitches.

12. **Corinthian Vine 12b/c**
    This demanding route ascends the smooth wall between the South Face and Never A Dull Moment. Begin with the right-facing dihedral of the South Face.

13. **Never a Dull Moment 12a s**
    An impressive route. Begin just to the right of the South Face route and angle up to the right, past two bolts, et cetera. Four pitches.

cave

CASTLE ROCK

6. **Cussin' Crack**   7
8. **Jackson's Wall**   6
11. **South Face**   9

14. **Athlete's Feat**   11a
16. **Country Club Crack**   11b/c
17. **Tourist's Extravaganza**   12d/13a

14. **Athlete's Feat   11a**

Classic. Begin at a pointed boulder just up and left from the bridge at the southeast corner of the rock. The crux of the route is a difficult mantel on the first pitch. Rack up to a #4 Friend.

15. **Englishman's Home   11b/c s**

Begin this ingenious and challenging route as for Athlete's Feat or Never a Dull Moment, but from the first belay, climb out to the right into a series of arched right-facing dihedrals. Three pitches.

16. **Country Club Crack   11b/c**

Classic hand crack. Begin atop a large block immediately right of Athlete's Feat. Two pitches.

17. **Tourist's Extravaganza   12d/13a**

Begin to the right of Country Club Crack and belay in a King Kong-sized solution pocket. Climb the steep wall up and right past a couple of bolts (crux) and belay in a recess with some alum root. Climb the crack.

18. **Radio Andromeda   11b**

Begin at the edge of the stream, a little way to the right of Tourist's Extravaganza and climb a system of black grooves (10b/c s). Make a short traverse left (11a) to a sling belay at two bolts and jam the awesome crack above (crux). Rack up to a #4 Friend.

Steve Ilg on Country Club Crack

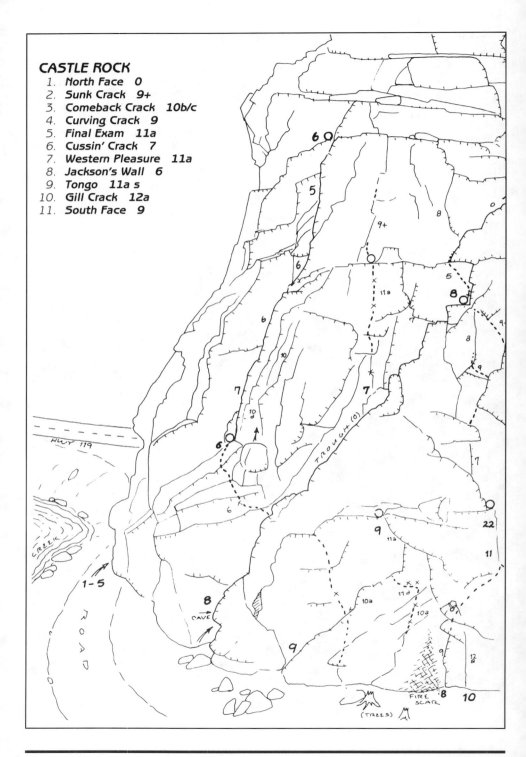

CASTLE ROCK
1. North Face 0
2. Sunk Crack 9+
3. Comeback Crack 10b/c
4. Curving Crack 9
5. Final Exam 11a
6. Cussin' Crack 7
7. Western Pleasure 11a
8. Jackson's Wall 6
9. Tongo 11a s
10. Gill Crack 12a
11. South Face 9

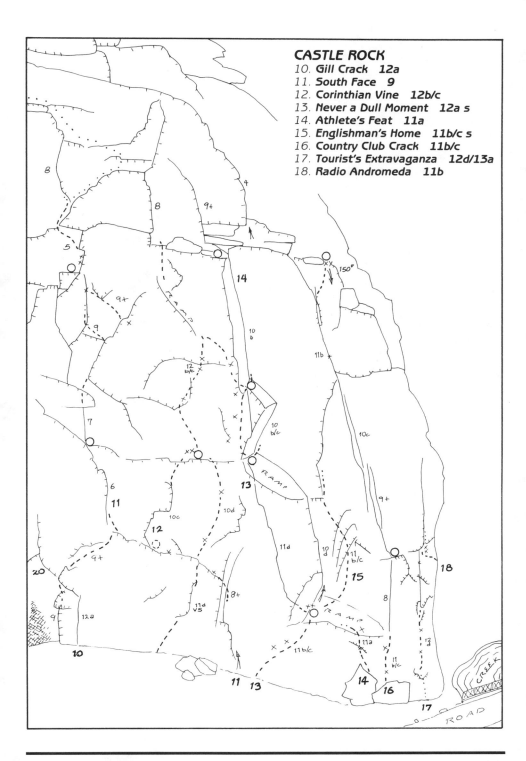

CASTLE ROCK

10. Gill Crack   12a
11. South Face   9
12. Corinthian Vine   12b/c
13. Never a Dull Moment   12a s
14. Athlete's Feat   11a
15. Englishman's Home   11b/c s
16. Country Club Crack   11b/c
17. Tourist's Extravaganza   12d/13a
18. Radio Andromeda   11b

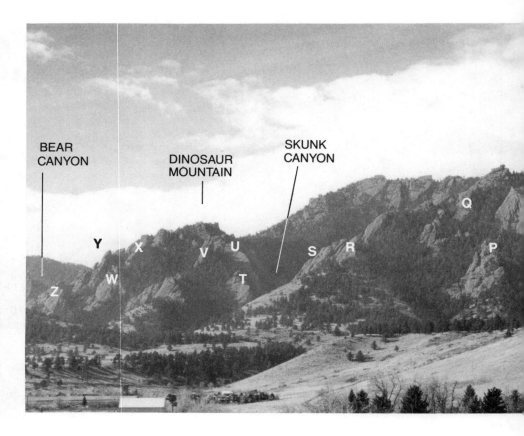

BEAR CANYON

DINOSAUR MOUNTAIN

SKUNK CANYON

Green Mountain

N Schmoe's Nose
O The Fifth Flatiron
P The Royal Arch
Q The Hour Glass
R The Hillbilly
S Satan's Slab
T Archean Pronouncement
U Dreadnaught
V The Backporch
W The Red Devil
X The Box
Y The Finger Flatiron
Z Der Zerkle

SUMMIT   BLUEBELL CANYON

Green Mountain

A   The First Flatiron
B   The SecondFlatiron
C   The Third Flatiron
D   Queen Anne's Head
E   W.C. Fields Pinnacle
F   East Ironing Board
G   West Ironing Board
H   The Thing
I   The Willy B.
J   The Spaceship
K   Green Mountain Pinnacle
L   The FourthFlatiron
M   Hammerhead
WQ Wood's Quarry

Green Mountain ─────────────────

THE BOUNDARIES OF BOULDER MOUNTAIN PARK enclose four large forested peaks. From north to south, they are Mount Sanitas (6,879 ft.), Flagstaff Mountain (6,950 ft), Green Mountain (8,144 ft.) and Boulder Mountain (8,549 ft). From downtown and the university area, Green Mountain is the most prominent of these and presents the characteristic view of the Flatirons for which the city has become famous. One finds here a wondrous and primitive environment waiting to be explored and appreciated. Enchanting trails wind in and out of the deep ravines, up the steep ridges and over the summit. Here, eagles and falcons soar, indifferent to the many human visitors. Along the broad eastern slope of the mountain, a cacophony of crags and slabs rise up above the dense forests in every imaginable shape and size. These are the Flatirons – a rock climber's paradise.

To reach the First through the Fifth Flatirons (the only ones that are numbered), go west on Baseline Road, or south on 9th Street to the intersection of the two. Go west one-half block and turn left into Chautauqua Park. If the Flatirons are not strikingly apparent from here, it is probably not a good day to go climbing. Hike up the old Kinnikinic Road (closed to autos), which leads south from the west side of the park, and find various trailheads in the vicinity of Bluebell Shelter, or begin with the Chautauqua Trail (see below).

TRAILS

The Mesa Trail runs on a north-south axis from Chautauqua Park to Eldorado Springs and is about six miles long. It branches left from Kinnikinic Road after about a quarter mile. It has two southern trailheads. See description under Bear Peak.

The Royal Arch Trail begins just south of Bluebell Shelter. It winds up Bluebell canyon beneath the Third Flatiron, climbs up to Sentinel Pass, and continues south to reach a rock formation called the Royal Arch after 0.9 mile.

The Chautauqua Trail begins just west of the ranger station in Chautauqua Park and leads southwest toward the First Flatiron, where it joins the Bluebell-Baird Trail after 0.6 mile. To reach the First Flatiron Trail or Bluebell Shelter, go left on the Bluebell-Baird Trail.

The First Flatiron Trail leads to the very base of the First Flatiron, then works up along the south edge of the face to the col between the First and Second Flatirons. A left branch after about the first 100 yards leads to the low point of the Second Flatiron and on around to the north to join the Third Flatiron Trail. The First Flatiron Trail cuts off to the west from the Bluebell-Baird Trail about midway between Bluebell Shelter and the junction with the Chautauqua Trail, which is to say, about 50 yards from either one.

The Third Flatiron Trail begins from the road just southwest of Bluebell Shelter. It heads west, then curves around to the south. After about 150 yards, it crosses a shallow draw. About 15 yards east of the draw, make a sharp right turn onto the new Third Flatiron Trail. About 30 yards after the trail crosses a talus field, the unmarked (why?) Second Flatiron Trail branches off to the right. About 50 yards beyond that junction, a left branch in the trail cuts across a second talus field and leads to the East Bench of the Third Flatiron. After this, the trail climbs steeply beneath the north face of the Third Flatiron and leads to the West Bench.

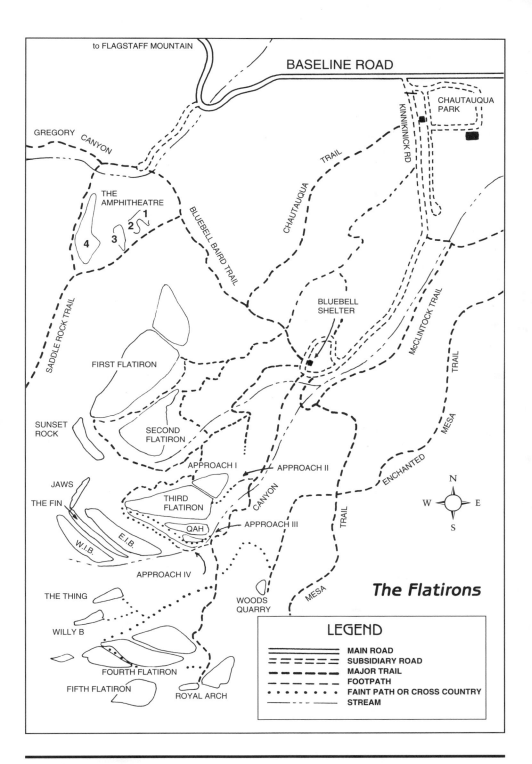

The Flatirons

LEGEND

———————	MAIN ROAD
= = = = =	SUBSIDIARY ROAD
▬ ▬ ▬ ▬ ▬	MAJOR TRAIL
– – – – –	FOOTPATH
• • • • • •	FAINT PATH OR CROSS COUNTRY
·–·–·–·	STREAM

to FLAGSTAFF MOUNTAIN

BASELINE ROAD

CHAUTAUQUA PARK

KINNIKINICK RD

GREGORY CANYON

CHAUTAUQUA TRAIL

THE AMPHITHEATRE

BLUEBELL BAIRD TRAIL

BLUEBELL SHELTER

McCLINTOCK TRAIL

SADDLE ROCK TRAIL

FIRST FLATIRON

SUNSET ROCK

SECOND FLATIRON

APPROACH I

APPROACH II

CANYON

MESA TRAIL

ENCHANTED

JAWS

THE FIN

THIRD FLATIRON

QAH

APPROACH III

E.I.B.

W.I.B.

APPROACH IV

THE THING

WILLY B

WOODS QUARRY

MESA

N
W · E
S

FOURTH FLATIRON

FIFTH FLATIRON

ROYAL ARCH

The NCAR Trail, combined with the Mallory Cave Trail, is the most common approach to Dinosaur Mountain. To reach the trailhead, take Table Mesa Drive west to NCAR (National Center for Atmospheric Research). The trail begins near the northwest corner of the parking area. It travels west over pleasant terrain, and meets the Mesa Trail in 0.5 mile. Note that this trail bifurcates into north and south branches about 50 yards before reaching the Mesa Trail.

Mallory Cave Trail. Note: the current Boulder Mountain Park Trail Map (1988) shows this trail going up a draw to the south of its actual location. The NCAR Trail splits before reaching the Mesa Trail; take the left (south) branch (not marked on the map), and from its junction with the Mesa Trail, pick up the Mallory Cave Trail. Follow the trail over a ridge into the next draw to the south, up past Square Rock – a large, free-standing boulder with good toproping – on to Der Zerkle, clockwise around to its west side, and north past the Hand to the base of the Finger Flatiron. To reach Mallory Cave, scramble up to the left in a diagonal groove, under or over a chockstone, up a slab – and voila, the cave.

Bear Canyon Trail. To reach the south side of Dinosaur Mountain, it is best to use the Bear Canyon Trail. This can be done from the NCAR approach by continuing south on the Mesa Trail to the service road in lower Bear Canyon, or more directly from a different trail head. See under Boulder Mountain.

FIRST FLATIRON

If not the most popular, certainly the most conspicuous crag in all the Boulder area is the First Flatiron. Its massive east face and castellated summit ridge dominate the northeast flank of Green Mountain. If the Third Flatiron draws more traffic, it is mainly because its Standard East Face Route is easier and less committing than its counterpart on the First. The Direct East Face route on the First Flatiron is one of the grand tours of Boulder climbing, and the view from the summit is the best of all the Flatirons.

Approach via the Chautauqua and First Flatiron Trails. To descend from the summit, downclimb the South Ridge route or rappel from large eyebolts that are fairly obvious on location. To return to the bottom of the east face, hike down the steep, wooded gully between the First and Second Flatirons. Or, head south a ways and find a more pleasant trail that drops down between the Second and Third Flatirons and joins the Third Flatiron Trail (see map).

1. **North Arete   4**
   This is a sweeping tour of the castellated skyline ridge. Begin with the Northeast Gully (below), or reach the traditional start by scrambling up around the right margin of the rock and mounting the ridge from the west as it rises out of the trees. Encounter several brief but entertaining uprisings enroute to the summit.

2. **Northeast Gully   5 s**
   Begin about one hundred feet up and right from the bottom of the face. Move out left and proceed up a shallow gully into a large, right-facing corner. Cross right to a tree, then back left to join the Direct East Face or the North Arete.

3. **Direct East Face   6 s**
   This is one of the finest east face routes in the Flatirons. Start early as the face is about 1,000 feet high, and some ten pitches are required to reach the summit. Begin from the very bottom of the face and proceed as shown in the topo. A fine variation climbs straight up a red slab from the first belay (6 s), over a small roof, and up an intimidating wide groove (9 s or 7 s just to the left).

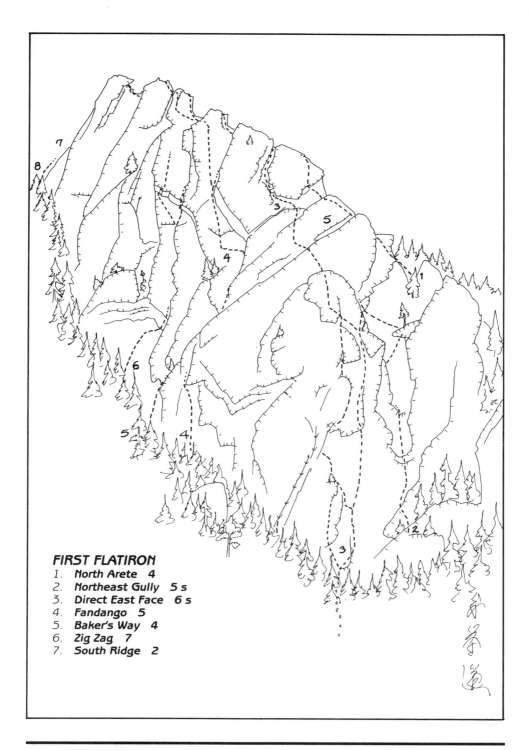

FIRST FLATIRON
1. **North Arete   4**
2. **Northeast Gully   5 s**
3. **Direct East Face   6 s**
4. **Fandango   5**
5. **Baker's Way   4**
6. **Zig Zag   7**
7. **South Ridge   2**

4. **Fandango 5**

One of the best routes on the First. Begin about 200 feet down to the right from Baker's Way or begin with that route. Follow a distinct left-facing system to the summit ridge. Look for a huge diagonal roof high on the wall.

5. **Baker's Way 4**

This is the easiest of the east face routes. Begin about halfway up along the south edge of the east face, below two small pines up on the wall. Climb a short, steep pitch up past the pines, then follow an easy ramp up and right across the face, all the way to the North Arete.

6. **Zig Zag 7**

Roll up for the mystery tour. Begin up and left from Baker's Way, climb a slab and follow a zig-zag, left-facing dihedral system to the top of the face.

7. **South Ridge 2**

This route provides the easiest unroped descent from the summit and is described from the top down. From the eyebolt on the summit, downclimb a short west-facing wall to a ledge. Drop down a groove to the south to another eyebolt, then downclimb the steep south face via obvious strata that descend toward the east. Or rappel from the eyebolts.

THIRD FLATIRON

"The Third," as it is known locally, rises abruptly and unmistakably from the forest slopes of Green Mountain and is beyond doubt the most popular of all the Flatirons. Visible from almost anywhere in Boulder, it has a peculiar prominence from the University of Colorado campus, and has (dare I say, thus) been the scene of various pranks and foolery. For example, it is the only flatiron to have been defaced by grafitti. A 100-foot-high "CU" has existed on the upper third of the east face for decades, and though scraped off, painted over, and camouflaged on various occasions, it was re-painted in dazzling white during the early 1980s. This monument to late puberty and "higher" education was again painted over so that hundreds of pounds of exterior latex now hang like a glacier above the city of Boulder, and it is possible to climb 100 feet of the east face without touching rock. The geological term flatiron is said to have been inspired by the crags of the Fountain Formation: the Third Flatiron, for its great size and distinctive shape, must have been at the heart of the idea.

All approaches are described beginning from Bluebell Shelter. See map.

Approach I leads to the Standard East Face Route and the West Bench via the Third Flatiron Trail (see above).

Approach II leads to the very bottom of the east face. Set out along the Royal Arch Trail for about three-tenths of a mile to a point just before it crosses to the left (south) side of Bluebell Canyon. Head steeply up to the southwest on a less-developed trail, stay to the left of a minor buttress, and arrive shortly at the nadir of the great face.

Approach III (the Inside Route) leads to the southwest face and the West Bench. The south side of 1911 Gully is formed by a massive, blocky ridge that begins with W.C. Fields Pinnacle and Queen Anne's Head and terminates a thousand feet higher at the top of Slip-Slide Ledge. The upper part of the ridge consists of two enormous buttresses that, from the east, appear as giant wedges stuffed between the top of Queen Anne's Head and the upper south face of the Third. These are referred to as the Inner and Outer Wedges. The ridge itself is known descriptively as the southeast ridge. The southwest face of this ridge gives rise to several interesting routes, including the Southwest Chimney, which is the easiest downclimb from the summit area.

The Inside Route follows a long ramp along the base of the ridge that runs all the way to the West Bench. To reach the ramp, hike the Royal Arch Trail to a point just beyond the east face. Here, a footpath leads down into the draw and up the other side to the bottom of the ramp, just south of W.C. Fields Pinnacle. Note that there are three short scrambles along this ramp. The first and most difficult, "the crux slab," is met about 500 feet above the stream crossing and ascends a northeast-facing bulge out of a grassy alcove. The second, about 200 feet further along, is a V- shaped section of slickrock below the Southwest Chimney. A final slab is encountered just below the West Bench. These three sections are trecherous when wet.

Approach IV (the Outside Route) leads to the West Bench by skirting around just below and to the south of Approach III. Take the Royal Arch Trail about 150 yards past W.C. Fields Pinnacle to the point where it begins to climb south out of Bluebell Canyon. Here, at a switchback to the left, is a large boulder with a painted sign that reads, "Royal Arch," with an arrow pointing left. Leave the main trail and contour west on a footpath. Cross the draw and hike up the wooded gully between the East Ironing Board and the cliffband of the Inside Route. At the top of the gully, scramble east over some big boulders and arrive at the West Bench and the steep west face of the Third Flatiron.

Descent from the summit: Make three rappels from large eyebolts. The direction and length of each rappel is stamped in a metal ring around the bolt. 1. Rappel 45 feet south from the summit to the South Bowl. 2. Rappel 50 feet south to Friday's Folly Ledge. Note that there are TWO eyebolts on this ledge. 3. Rappel 140 feet south from the eastern bolt and land near the top of Approach III, or move west on the ledge and rappel 72 feet west to reach the West Bench at the bottom of Friday's Folly route. It is also possible to downclimb the Southwest Chimney route (see below).

The routes are listed clockwise around the crag, beginning with the north side of the east face. Routes on Queen Anne's Head and W.C. Fields Pinnacle are not given.

THIRD FLATIRON – East Face

Use Approach I.

1. **College Drop-Out   7 s or 8 s**
   An unorthodox alternative to the standard east face curriculum – with lots of good climbing. Begin from a bench with trees about 75 feet up and right from the East Bench. Climb about 75 feet up a large right-facing dihedral and belay at a small tree. Continue up the corner for about 100 feet and exit at alflake on the left (6) – or continue up the dihedral and climb the well-protected PhD Roof (11a) to gain the main east face. Follow the right edge of the face to the summit. One may also climb straight up from the East Bench.

2. **Extra Point   6 s**
   This line parallels Drop-Out on the left. Six pitches.

3. **Standard East Face Route   4 s**
   This is probably the best beginner climb in the solar system. Begin from the East Bench. In brief, the line angles up and left past the first of six large eyebolts, traverses left across a wide groove or channel, then climbs more or less straight up past the five remaining bolts to the bottom of a deep cleft called the Gash. From here, the original route moves up and left to the South Bowl, then out onto the east face via Kiddy Kar Ledge, and on to the summit. One also may climb the face to the

THIRD FLATIRON – East Face
1. **College Drop-Out   7 s or 8 s**
3. **Standard East Face Route   4 s**
4. **East Face Left   5 s**

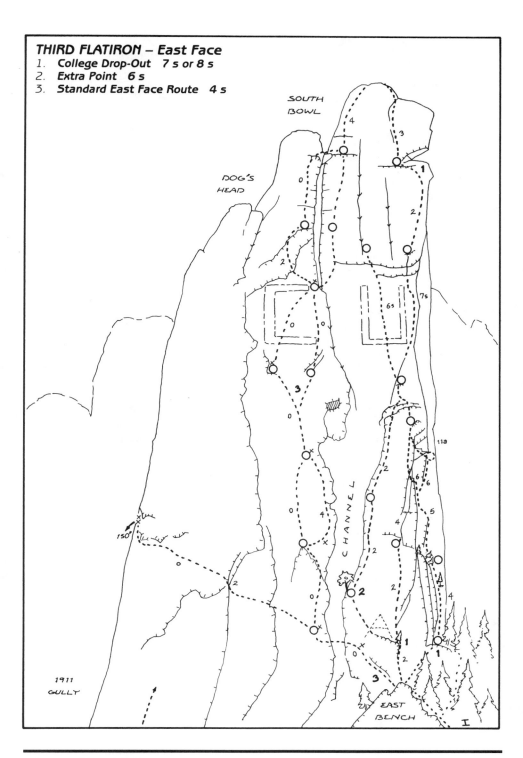

THIRD FLATIRON – East Face

1. *College Drop-Out*   7 s or 8 s
2. *Extra Point*   6 s
3. *Standard East Face Route*   4 s

SOUTH
BOWL

DOG'S
HEAD

CHANNEL

150'

1911
GULLY

EAST
BENCH

right of the cleft straight up to the summit (recommended). Or, for those inclined to spelunking, the Gash itself may be climbed past a couple of chockstones to the South Bowl.

4. **East Face Left   5 s**

This is the longest route in the Boulder area. Use Approach II. From the very bottom of the face, climb a blunt rib that angles up to the right to where it fades. Then, climb directly toward the left side of a long overhang that is passed on the left – or climb a crack through its middle (7). Climb up and right for a long way, and join the Standard East Face Route at the South Bowl.

THIRD FLATIRON – South Face

The following four routes are on the smooth, vertical, south-facing wall that forms the right side of 1911 Gully. Take Approach I to the East Bench, then scramble up and left across the east face to its south edge. Rappel into 1911 Gully from a two-bolt anchor at the top of Shoyu State.

5. **Sayonara   9 or 11b/c**

This is the furthest east of the four routes. Follow a line of bolts to the same fate as Blazing Biners. An easier start climbs straight up to the fourth bolt and requires a #0.5, 1, and 1.5 Friend for the initial roof.

6. **Blazing Biners   10a**

Bu-rei-zin-gu bi-na-ru in Japanese. From the fern garden in 1911 Gully, make a few moves to get up into a five-foot wide slot, place pro in a one-inch crack underneath the roof and swing up onto the face at a good hold. Climb straight up past three bolts to a narrow ledge (75 feet). Rappel from slings around a horn or climb 20 feet (6) up onto the east face to escape.

7. **Shoyu State   11a**

This 100-foot pitch provides fine, vertical face climbing on pebbles and rugosities that is unlike anything else on the Third Flatiron. Begin on a ramp at the upper end of a large, diagonal slot. Master a bulge and follow a line of bolts up and left. And no, Shoyu State is not a Japanese university.

8. **South Face   10d s**

An old aid route. Begin beneath an arching roof/dihedral, high on the wall.

Southeast Ridge

The following routes begin from the long ramp of Approach III.

9. **Holier Than Thou   11b**
   This is a bolt line up the overhanging pocketed wall just up the approach ramp from W.C. Fields Pinnacle. No topo. 5 bolts and a pin.

10. **South Chimney   5**
    The South Chimney actually is a huge fault between the Inner and Outer Wedges that cuts all the way through the southeast ridge to 1911 Gully. Begin in a large right-facing dihedral about 30 feet above the "crux slab" of Approach III.

11. **Rite of Spring   9**
    This route ascends the steep, 250-foot south face of the Inner Wedge. Begin on a buttress, about eight feet left of a cave and to the left of the South Chimney. Climb up about 60 feet and belay on a ramp beneath a pocketed overhang with a bolt. Climb up past the bolt and aim for a small dihedral and thin crack high on the wall.

12. **The Southwest Chimney   4**
    This is the easiest downclimb from the summit, as well as a nice moderate route. Begin at a good ledge just above the "V" section of Approach III. Climb the chimney past a large chockstone (crux) and belay from a large eyebolt. Scramble west up Slip-Slide Ledge, enter the South Bowl via Fatman's Frenzy, cross the top of the Gash, traverse out onto the main east face, and climb straight to the summit.

13. **The Winky Woo   4**
    Begin just left of the Southwest Chimney. Angle up and left on large holds to reach Fat Man's Frenzy in two pitches. Rack up to a #4 Friend.

14. **Waiting for Columbus   10c**
    This long, sustained pitch ascends the dead-vertical buttress at the right of Pentaprance. Begin on a ledge about 30 feet up and about 150 feet east from the top of Approach III. Climb short cracks, pockets, a cool roof, et cetera. Belay from a horn on Slip-Slide Ledge. 165 feet, 5 bolts. Standard rack.

15. **Pentaprance   10d s**
    A curious name. Climb the awesome, left-facing dihedral just left of Waiting for Columbus.

THIRD FLATIRON – West Face

Use Approach I, III, or IV to reach the West Bench; Approach I is recommended.

16. **Friday's Folly   7**
    A Boulder classic. Begin just left of the arete formed by the right edge of the west face. Follow a crack up and around the arete onto the south face and zigzag up obvious terrain to Friday's Folly Ledge. From here, one can rappel or continue straight up to the summit via the exciting and exposed Direct Finish (7). See topo.

17. **Saturday's Folly   8+**
    A fine, steep route that climbs the imposing face to the left of the northwest arete. Begin about 12 feet left of Friday's Folly, near some chopped bolts. The 75-foot pitch ends at Friday's Folly Ledge.

SOUTH BOWL

DOG'S HEAD

WEST BENCH

17

16

15

14

12

13

APPROACH IV

APROACH III

THIRD FLATIRON – Upper Southwest Face

12. **The Southwest Chimney   4**
13. **The Winky Woo   4**
14. **Waiting for Columbus   10c**

15. **Pentaprance   10d s**
16. **Friday' s Folly   7**
17. **Saturday' s Folly   8+**

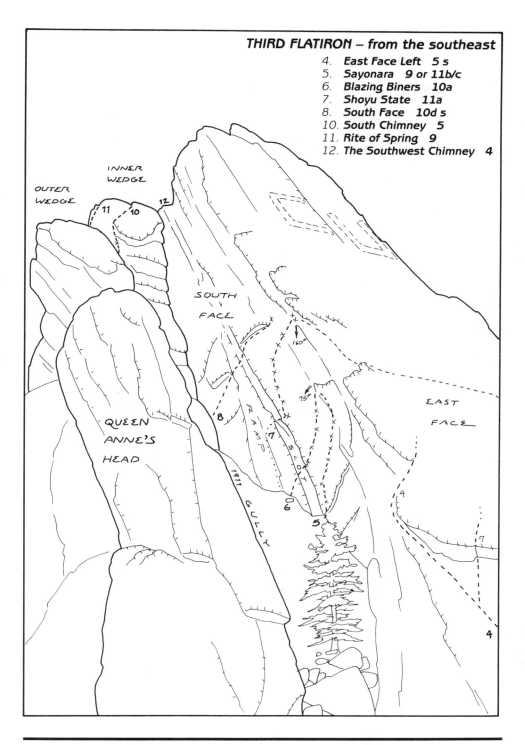

THIRD FLATIRON – from the southeast

4. **East Face Left** 5 s
5. **Sayonara** 9 or 11b/c
6. **Blazing Biners** 10a
7. **Shoyu State** 11a
8. **South Face** 10d s
10. **South Chimney** 5
11. **Rite of Spring** 9
12. **The Southwest Chimney** 4

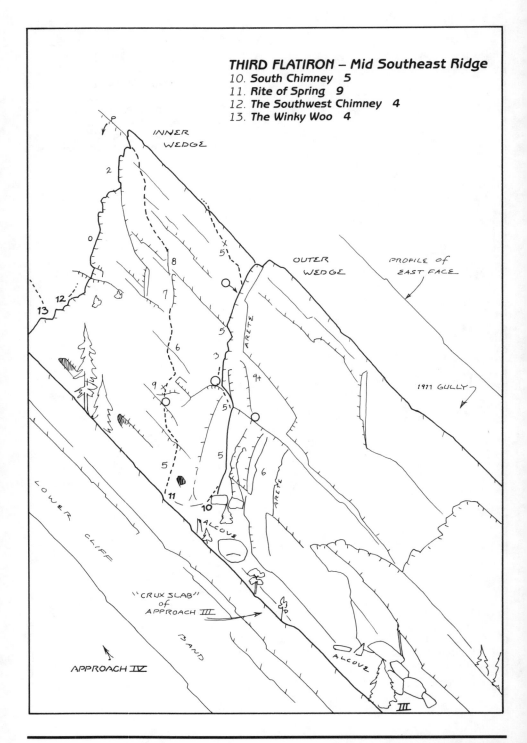

THIRD FLATIRON – Mid Southeast Ridge
10. **South Chimney** 5
11. **Rite of Spring** 9
12. **The Southwest Chimney** 4
13. **The Winky Woo** 4

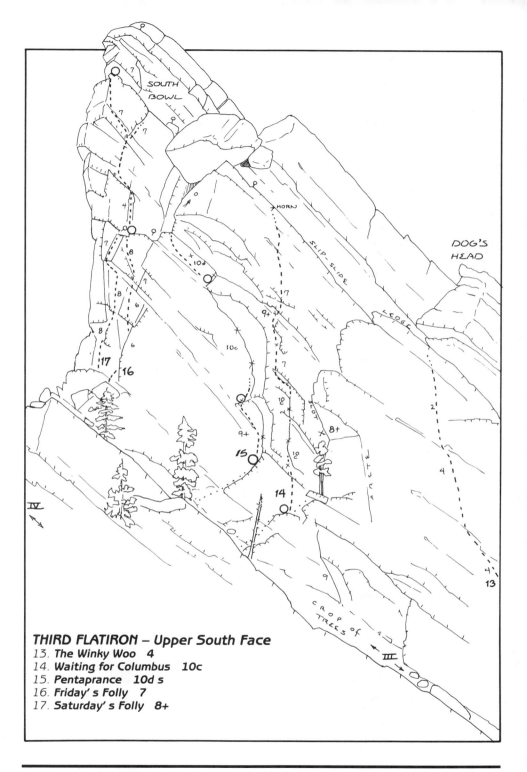

SOUTH
BOWL

HORN

SLIP-SLIDE

DOG'S
HEAD

LEDGE

SLOT

ARÊTE

CROP of TREES

THIRD FLATIRON – Upper South Face
13. *The Winky Woo* 4
14. *Waiting for Columbus* 10c
15. *Pentaprance* 10d s
16. *Friday' s Folly* 7
17. *Saturday' s Folly* 8+

17   16   15   14   13

IRONING BOARDS

Just souhwest of the Third Flatiron two magnificnet slabs arch up to the north from Bluebell Canyon and terminate along the crest of a wooded ridge. The lower slab, nearer to the Third, is the East Ironing Board; the further is the West Ironing Board. A long, graceful blade of rock called The Fin rises in parallel fashion between the two. Only the East Ironing Board is described with selected routes on the west and southwest faces.

Use Approach IV for the Third Flatiron and hike around the bottom of the East Ironing Board after leaving the Royal Arch Trail. One may also reach west side routes by hiking west along the north side of the ridge crest from the West Bench of the Third Flatiron. This is especially useful for reaching routes on or near the Green Thumb.

Descent. From the level section of the ridge crest, just south of a large vertical step, rappel 50 feet west into the gully between The Fin and the west face. Or, one may also downclimb or rappel down a groove for 80 feet (east) to a tree, then rappel 150 feet to the gully of Approach IV.

Green Thumb is the blunt tower at the north end of the East Ironing Board. The first two routes ascend its west side. To escape from the summit, scramble south and rappel west from a tree. Routes 3 through 11 are to the right (south) along the west face.

1. **Green Corner 9**
   Climb the obvious crack at the northwest corner of the buttress.

2. **Farniente 12a**
   Pinch pebbles up the vertical west face. Six bolts and a two-bolt anchor.

3. **Green Crack 8+**
   Climb the clean, south-facing dihedral at the right (south) side of Green Thumb.

4. **Diagonal Finger Crack 9**
   A little beauty. Jam the diagonal crack to the right of Green Crack.

5. **Zimbra 12b**
   Seven bolts about 60 feet right from Farniente.

6. **The Raven 11c**
   A steep, left-facing dihedral about 200 feet down and to the right from the Green Thumb. Rappel 50 feet west from two bolts. The dihedral to the right is rated 9.

7. **The Stars at Noon 12d**
   Stem about half-way up the dihedral of The Raven, then move out right (crux) and climb the arete.

8. **Sinatra's World 13a**
   Follow a line of bolts that goes straight up from the start to Slave to the Rhythm. Six bolts to a two-bolt anchor.

9. **Slave to the Rhythm 13b**
   This improbable line features very strenuous, overhanging climbing on huecos, pebbles, and thin edges. Begin immediately right of the dihedral to the right of Raven. Eight bolts to a two-bolt anchor.

10. **Velvet Elvis 11a**
    An unusual and exhilerating route. Begin about 300 feet up from the south end of the crag, beneath a left-arching dihedral. Climb a roof with a fixed pin, then traverse left just above the roof to an anchor. The crux second pitch goes up to the ridge crest.

11. **Hammer of Thor 10c**
    From the second bolt on Velvet Elvis, work up to the ridge crest past five bolts. Rack: 8 QD.

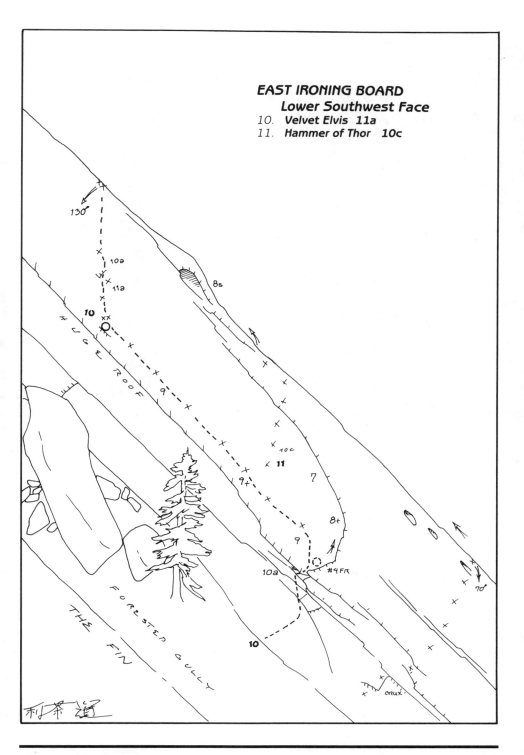

EAST IRONING BOARD
Lower Southwest Face
10. Velvet Elvis 11a
11. Hammer of Thor   10c

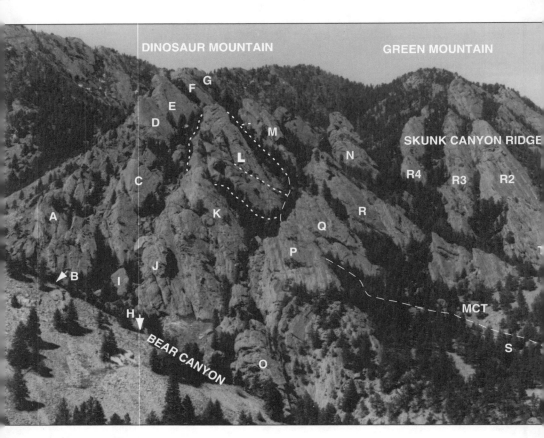

Skunk Canyon, North Side

R1 **Ridge One**
R2 **Ridge Two**

R3 **Ridge Three**
R4 **Ridge Four**

Skunk Canyon, South Side (Dinosaur Mountain)

A **Achean Pronouncement**
B **Dreadnaught Ridge**

C **North Ridge**
MCT **Mallory Cave Trail**

Bear Canyon, North Side (Dinosaur Mountain)

A **South Ridge**
B **Stonehenge**
C **Fee**
D **Fi**
E **Fo**
F **Fum**
G **Dum**
H **Southern Dinosaur Egg**
I **The Bubble**
J **Northern Dinosaur Egg**

K **Der Freischutz**
L **Finger Flatiron**
M **The Box**
N **The Back Porch**
O **Bear Creek Spire**
P **Dinosaur Rock**
Q **Der Zerkle**
R **Red Devil**
S **Square Rock**
T. **The Front Porch**

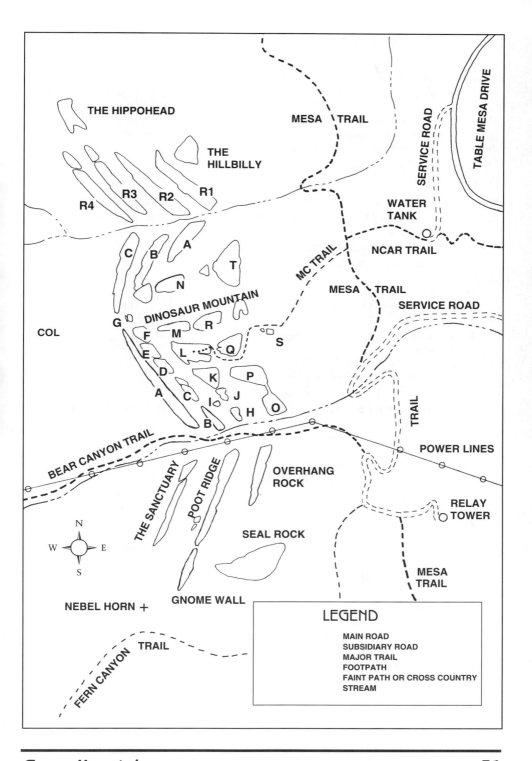

THE HIPPOHEAD

MESA TRAIL

SERVICE ROAD

TABLE MESA DRIVE

THE HILLBILLY

R1

R2

R3

R4

WATER TANK

MC TRAIL

NCAR TRAIL

C B A

T

N

MESA TRAIL

SERVICE ROAD

DINOSAUR MOUNTAIN

COL

G

F M R

E L Q S

D

A C K P

I J

B H O

TRAIL

BEAR CANYON TRAIL

POWER LINES

THE SANCTUARY

POOT RIDGE

OVERHANG ROCK

RELAY TOWER

N
W E
S

SEAL ROCK

MESA TRAIL

NEBEL HORN +

GNOME WALL

FERN CANYON TRAIL

LEGEND

MAIN ROAD
SUBSIDIARY ROAD
MAJOR TRAIL
FOOTPATH
FAINT PATH OR CROSS COUNTRY
STREAM

DINOSAUR MOUNTAIN

DINOSAUR MOUNTAIN RISES majestically between Skunk Canyon on the north and Bear Canyon on the south. It is a satellite peak of Green Mountain and is one of the most beautiful and complex features in the Boulder range. The most popular destination on Dinosaur Mountain is (or was) Mallory Cave, which lies between the Hand and the Finger Flatiron. But the cave has been upstaged by the development of numerous high-quality climbing routes. Good slab climbing is encountered on the east faces of some of the formations, whereas the steep south and west sides present some of the best modern face climbs in the Flatirons.

DER ZERKLE

Der Zerkle is a fairly large flatiron that sits near the middle of the east face of Dinosaur Mountain. The Mallory Cave Trail brings one along the south and west sides of the crag and provides easy access to the routes. To descend from the summit, downclimb the northwest side of the crag past a big tree.

The Court is an alcove at the southwest corner of Der Zerkle with the following three routes. No topos.

1. **Knot Carrot   11a**
   Follow the right of two lines of bolts on the steep west face of The Court.
2. **Touch Monkey   11b**
   Follow a line of bolts just left of Knot Carrot.
3. **April Fools   10d**
   Follow a line of bolts up the bulging wall to the left from Touch Monkey. Lower off. Rack: #1 Tricam, small wires, 4 QD.

As the Mallory Cave Trail curves around the west face of Der Zerkle, encounter a "wall of huecos" with several bolt routes (8 to 11c, left to right) and a crack climb near the center (8+).

THE BOX

This steep and narrow crag lies about 200 feet north of the Finger Flatiron. Although relatively small, it is easily recognized from many locations by its summit tower, which resembles the dorsal fin of a shark. This is not to be confused with the small, phallic pinnacle above Mallory Cave that is called the Shark' s Fin, but doesn' t look like one. The upper south face of The Box is a very smooth, slightly concave wall of unusual beauty that is host to a pair of excellent routes. Approach via the Mallory Cave Trail. From its end beneath the Finger Flatiron, follow a new climber' s trail northwest into a wooded gully, then west to the notch between the Finger Flatiron and the Box. In addition to the routes described below, there are a couple of good face climbs around on the upper north face of the Box.

1. **Discipline   12b**
   Another victory over boredom and poor taste. Begin at the low point of the concave face. Stick-clip the first bolt. Rack: 6 QD; one also may use a #3.5 or 4 Friend in a hole above the second bolt and a small TCU near the top.
2. **Cornucopia   12d**
   Begin from the top of a large boulder just left of Discipline. Five bolts. Sadly, the bolts have been placed such that "cheater slings," which mar the beauty of the face, are needed to facilitate clip-ins.

THE BOX
1. **Discipline 12b**
2. **Cornucopia 12d**

THE FINGER FLATIRON

This is the long, narrow flatiron at the end of the Mallory Cave Trail. The following west side routes are encountered on the hike between The Box and The Hand/Der Freischutz area. Also, the far right side of the east face provides a fine slab route (7). Approach as for The Box and hike south from the top of the trail.

1. **Nude Figures in a Hollow Fruit   11a**
   Ascend the clean, 50-foot face past two roofs and three bolts at the far west side of the north face.

2. **Monodoigt   11c**
   Begin from the talus directly beneath the west arete of the summit tower. Climb a smooth, concave face past three bolts.

3. **Quest for Balance   11b**
   Begin about 100 feet down the gully from Monodoigt, in a stand of trees at the left of the path. Climb the southwest-facing buttress past five bolts.

THE HAND

This amorphous crag is south of the Finger Flatiron and north of Der Freischutz. The east face is rather lumpy and undistinguished but the steep south and west faces have some good routes. Approach via the Mallory Cave Trail, which passes the bottom of the east face just before reaching the Finger Flatiron. From the southeast corner of the rock, follow a path up a wooded gully into the alcove between the south face of The Hand and the north face of Der Freischutz. Lower off from all routes.

1. **Back in Slacks   11c**
   This is the furthest east of the bolt routes on the south face and the first encountered on the approach. Climb overhanging pockets to the right of Power Bulge. Four bolts.

2. **Power Bulge   12b/c**
   This very strenuous route takes the center of the imposing bulge just left of Back in Slacks. Five bolts.

Reach the following routes by scrambling up a smooth ramp beneath the overhanging west face.

3. **The Perfect Kiss 11d – Rock Atrocity   13d**
   Climb a line of six bolts at the southwest corner of The Hand (11d). This is about 50 feet to the left of Power Bulge. Climb the large roof past nine bolts (13d).

4. **Father on Fire   10d**
   Crack with three bolts to the left of the Perfect Kiss.

5. **New Saigon   11a**
   Farthest north of the bolt routes on the west face. The first clip-in is difficult. Three bolts.

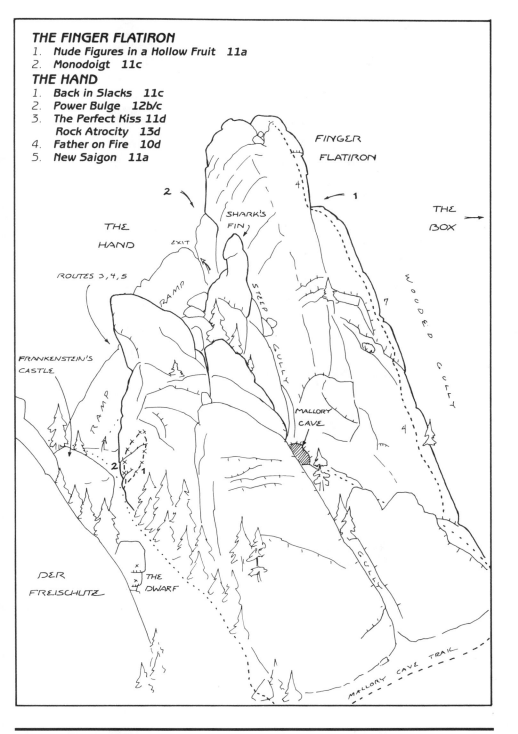

THE FINGER FLATIRON
1. Nude Figures in a Hollow Fruit 11a
2. Monodoigt 11c

THE HAND
1. Back in Slacks 11c
2. Power Bulge 12b/c
3. The Perfect Kiss 11d
   Rock Atrocity 13d
4. Father on Fire 10d
5. New Saigon 11a

FINGER FLATIRON

THE HAND

THE BOX

ROUTES 3,4,5

SHARK'S FIN

EXIT

RAMP

STEEP GULLY

WOODED GULLY

FRANKENSTEIN'S CASTLE

RAMP

MALLORY CAVE

DER FREISCHUTZ

THE DWARF

GULLY

MALLORY CAVE TRAIL

Greg Robinson at the first bolt on Discipline, The Box

DER FREISCHUTZ

Der Freischutz is the quaint little flatiron just south of The Hand. It is distinguished by good scrambling on its south and east sides and by two excellent bolt routes on its west face. Approach as for the south face of the Hand. Once below Power Bulge, head southwest across the wooded alcove and arrive shortly at the northwest arete.

1. **Bidoigt   10a**
   Begin on a big boulder at the base of the northwest arete. Work up past two bolts and a short, thin crack. A mid-range TCU and a 3# RP are useful.

2. **Drugs   11b**
   Follow a line of four bolts about 15 feet to the right of Bidoigt.

THE HAND & FINGER FLATIRON   STONEHENGE

SOUTHERN DINOSAUR EGG

This strange rock rises right out of Bear Creek, just east of Stonehenge. Approach as for Stonehenge, or hike south from the west side of Der Freischutz. To descend from the summit, rappel 60 feet down the southwest face from the bolts at the top of Sneak Preview.

1. **Hatch 6**

   Climb a crack and chimney for a full rope length up the east face to the top of a large, flat-topped chockstone, then straight up the steep south face to the summit (crux).

2. **Sneak Preview 11c**

   Follow a line of six bolts up the very steep southwest face.

STONEHENGE

Stonehenge rises directly from Bear Creek as a clean, narrow buttress; it stretches to the north for about 300 feet, then ends abruptly in a stand of trees. The steeple-shaped south face is visible through the trees to the north a short way before the Bear Canyon Trail crosses the creek.

1. **Thought Control 9**

   This short but wonderful route ascends the steeple-shaped south face. Four bolts with the crux above the second.

2. **Auspice 11d**

   Begin beneath the southwest face, 50 feet above the creek. Turn a roof and follow a line of four bolts up a smooth and beautiful face. One may continue up the easier but unprotected face above the fourth bolt to a two-bolt anchor (85 feet).

3. **The Fiend 13b**

   On the west face, about 200 feet above the creek, climb a yellow, right-facing dihedral above an overhang. Four bolts and a pin. Bring a #1 and 2 Friend or equivalent.

There are two worthwhile routes on the South Ridge – the next feature west from Stonehenge. Follow the trail around to the west side of the last long ridge and hike about 150 yards up the slope. Look for two bolt routes just right of a juniper tree. No topo.

1. **Liquid Crystal 11c**

   This is the line on the right. Five bolts to a two-bolt anchor.

2. **Megasaurus 11a**

   This is the line on the left. Four bolts up to the same anchor as above.

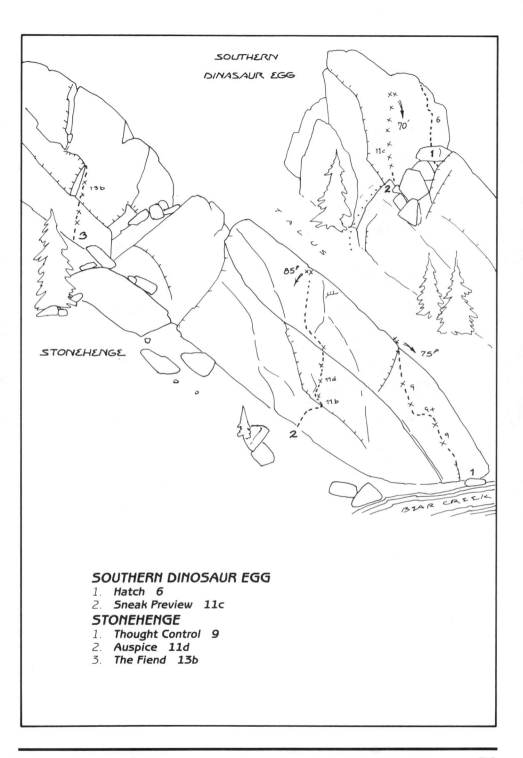

SOUTHERN DINOSAUR EGG
1. **Hatch   6**
2. **Sneak Preview   11c**

STONEHENGE
1. **Thought Control   9**
2. **Auspice   11d**
3. **The Fiend   13b**

Boulder Mountain from the northeast

A   South Pinnacle
B   Stonehenge
C   Poot Ridge
D   Gnome Wall
E   Overhang Rock
F   Harmon Cave
G   Seal Rock
H   The Goose
I   Southern Goose Egg
HCT Harmon Cave Trail
FCT Fern Canyon Trail
FC   Fern Canyon

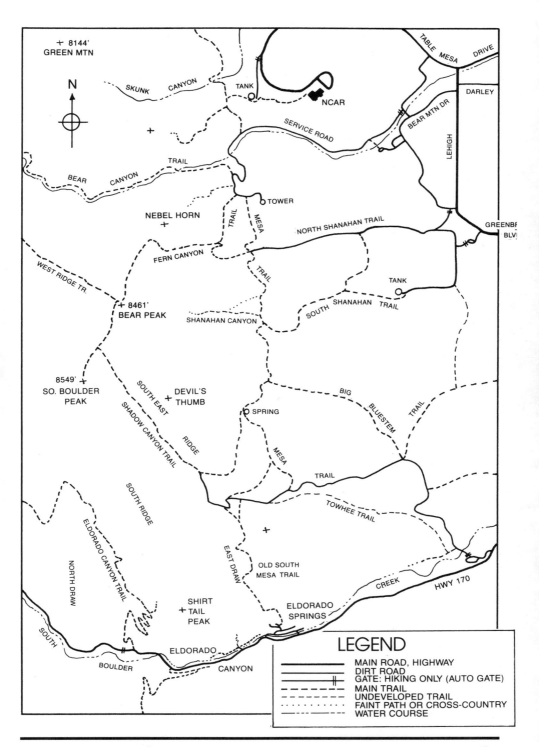

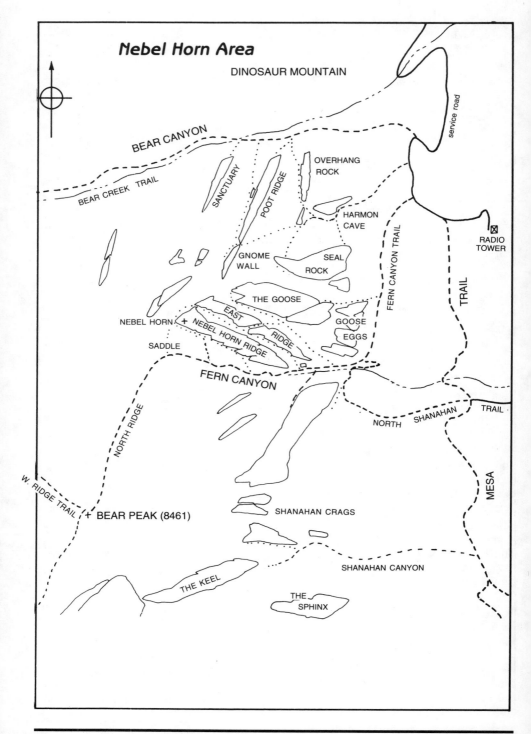

Nebel Horn Area

DINOSAUR MOUNTAIN

BEAR CANYON

BEAR CREEK TRAIL

SANCTUARY

POOT RIDGE

OVERHANG ROCK

HARMON CAVE

GNOME WALL

SEAL ROCK

THE GOOSE

NEBEL HORN

EAST RIDGE

NEBEL HORN RIDGE

GOOSE EGGS

SADDLE

FERN CANYON TRAIL

Service road

RADIO TOWER

TRAIL

FERN CANYON

NORTH RIDGE

NORTH SHANAHAN TRAIL

MESA

W. RIDGE TRAIL

BEAR PEAK (8461)

SHANAHAN CRAGS

SHANAHAN CANYON

THE KEEL

THE SPHINX

Boulder Mountain————————————

THE SKYLINE TO THE SOUTH of Green Mountain is graced by the tapering rocky summit of Bear Peak (8,461 ft.). This is the northern twin of double-summited Boulder Mountain, which lies between Bear Canyon and Eldorado Canyon; the southern and higher summit is South Boulder Peak (8,549 ft.). Just across Bear Canyon from Dinosaur Mountain, the craggy subsidiary summit of the Nebel Horn rises up along the northeast shoulder of Bear Peak. This large, forested dome is separated from the main peak by a broad, sandy col that marks the top of Fern Canyon. The Nebel Horn – which features the major crags of Fern Canyon – offers excellent climbing that includes classic slabs and numerous modern face climbs protected by bolts.

TRAILS

For those pallid waifs who disdain walking, it will be better to move on to the next chapter, as Boulder Mountain offers no drive-up crags, and the nearest routes are at least a 30-minute hike from the road.

The Mesa Trail runs on a north-south axis all along the east side of Green Mountain and Boulder Mountain and is crossed or traveled upon in the approaches to all the crags in this chapter. The Mesa Trail along Bear Peak may be reached from the Bear Creek service road, Shanahan Trail, the new south section of the Mesa Trail, or the Old Mesa Trail from Eldorado Springs. Only the first two options are of use for routes described in this book.

Bear Canyon Trail affords access to the north slope of the Nebel Horn and to the south slope of Dinosaur Mountain. To reach the trailhead from Broadway, go west on Table Mesa Drive, left (south) on Lehigh Street, right (west) on Bear Mountain Drive, and right on Stoney Hill Road to a cul de sac at its end. Park here, find the trail through a wooden gate, cross Bear Creek, and hike west on a service road for about 0.7 mile to its junction with the Mesa Trail. Continue on the service road (here the Mesa Trail) for another half mile as it winds around to the south. Find the Bear Canyon Trail at a switchback below some powerlines.

Harmon Cave Trail. This unmarked trail provides relatively easy access to Seal Rock and Gnome Wall. Its beginning is indistinct and lurches up to the west from the service road (Mesa Trail) about midway between the cut-offs to the Bear Canyon Trail and the Fern Canyon Trail. See map.

The Fern Canyon Trail may be used to approach the Goose, Fern Canyon and the summit of Bear Peak. Reach this trail via the Bear Creek service road (see Bear Canyon Trail) or the north branch of the Shanahan Trail (below). From the Bear Creek service road, continue north on the Mesa Trail about 60 yards past the Bear Canyon Trail to the signed trailhead on the right. It is about one mile from here to the col at the top of Fern Canyon.

Shanahan Trail (north branch). This is the most efficient approach to Fern Canyon. From South Broadway, turn west on Greenbriar Drive, continue for about a mile, and turn left on Hardscrabble Drive. At the west end of this street is a circle with a few parking slots. Hike west from here as shown in the map. The trail leads directly beneath the northeast corner of The Slab and in another 50 yards, intersects the Fern Canyon Trail, 1.5 miles. For reasons unknown, the section of this trail between the Mesa Trail and Fern Canyon Trail is not shown on the Boulder Mountain Park Trail Map (1988), nor is it signed at either end.

NEBEL HORN

The following crags are on the Nebel Horn, the beautiful forested dome on the northeast shoulder of Bear Peak between Bear Canyon and Fern Canyon.

OVERHANG ROCK

This narrow, serrated crag is located just above the Bear Canyon Trail on the north slope of the Nebel Horn. Once across from Stonehenge (see Dinosaur Mountain), break off to the south on a steep path that leads to the talus field beneath the expansive west face.

1. **Snake Watching   13a**
   A spectacular route. Begin beneath an overhang at far left side of the west face. 150 feet, 15 bolts.

2. **Tits Out For The Lads   12b**
   This is the left of three bolt routes in the middle of the west face. Proceed from a ledge 30 feet above the talus that is formed by a huge flake. Seven bolts, 80 feet.

3. **The Big Picture   12a**
   This is the middle of three routes that begin atop a huge flake midway along the base of the west face. Eight bolts, 80 feet.

4. **The Missing Link   12b/c**
   Begin 20 feet to the right of the Big Picture and follow a line of six bolts. Lower off.

5. **Name Unknown   11d**
   This is yet another bolt route about 20 feet to the right of Missing Link.

SEAL ROCK

On the northeast slope of the Nebel Horn, Seal Rock towers above the trees and dominates the landscape. Its great east and north faces are visible from almost anywhere in Boulder and offer some unusual and very dramatic climbing.

Approach via the Harmon Cave Trail. To reach the bottom of the east face, hike past Harmon Cave and head south once in line with a huge boulder in the trees on the left (south). To reach the north face, continue up the trail to where a slab rises up on the left. Follow the path along the base of the slab, then angle around to the west into a talus field. From here, the north face towers above the trees and leaves little need for map and compass. Work west a bit, then up to the bottom of the face.

Descent. Rappel 165 feet to the north from a bolt anchor at the top of the Sea of Joy. Be prepared for a short downclimb at the bottom. It is also possible, though tedious, to downclimb the Shortcut (4).

1. **East Face Right   4**
   A Flatiron classic that combines solid rock with exhilarating exposure. Begin at the low point of the east face and follow its far right (north) edge all the way to the summit. About two- thirds of the way up, the Shortcut leads off north into the trees – a convenient escape, if needed. The angle steepens above this point and the best climbing on the route is encountered. Stay hard to the right edge, or work left about 30 feet and climb a beautiful, 100-foot-long finger crack (2) to the final slabs.

2. **Shortcut   4**
   This is the easiest way to reach the summit. Approach as for the north face. Walk left (east) beneath the high, vertical aspect of the north face until it is obvious to scramble up onto the north edge of the east face.

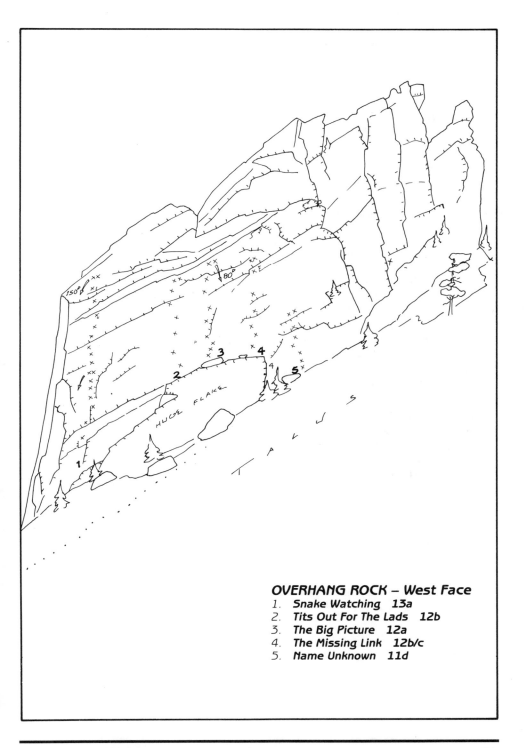

OVERHANG ROCK – West Face

1. Snake Watching   13a
2. Tits Out For The Lads   12b
3. The Big Picture   12a
4. The Missing Link   12b/c
5. Name Unknown   11d

3. **Sea of Joy   13a**
   See cover photo. This is a spectacular and well-protected route up the center of the
   north face. From the bottom of the face, scramble up a ramp to the right and belay
   on a bench directly below the black water streak on the hanging headwall. Three
   pitches. Rack: 8 QDs and a couple runners for the belays. It is possible to rappel
   from the top and do just the last pitch.

4. **Archaeopteryx   11c/d vs**
   This route, named for the earliest known avian, parallels Sea of Joy on the right.
   Three pitches. Rack up to a #3.5 Friend.

THE GOOSE

About 200 feet to the south of Seal Rock, at the margin of Fern Canyon, stands another
massive flatiron. That it in any way resembles a goose is a matter of speculation.
Approach via the Fern Canyon Trail. To reach the south and west faces, hike about 50
yards past the narrow entrance to the canyon, then scramble north (right) up open forest
and talus between the Goose and the East Ridge (the easterly of the two rock strata on
the north side of Fern Canyon). Descend via rappel or downclimb from the notch
between the two summits. No topo.

1. **Sweet and Innocent   10a**
   Begin with a left-facing dihedral in the upper south face. Two pitches.

2. **Wild Horses   13a**
   A spectacular route. Begin as for Sweet and Innocent, but break left out of the
   dihedral and follow a line of bolts over a bulging headwall. Rappel 145 feet. Rack
   up to a #1.5 Friend, plus 10 QDs.

3. **Raging Bull   11a or 12b/c**
   Steep and strenuous. The first pitch is fairly popular. Begin on a pedestal near the
   left edge of the south face and follow a line of bolts to a big ledge (11a). The second
   pitch works up and right over the bulging headwall. Rappel 165 feet. Rack: 8 QDs
   and wired stoppers.

4. **Deserted Cities of the Heart   9**
   Follow bolts up the center of the smooth northwest face. Another bolt route lies to
   the left (10a). Both routes are quite good.

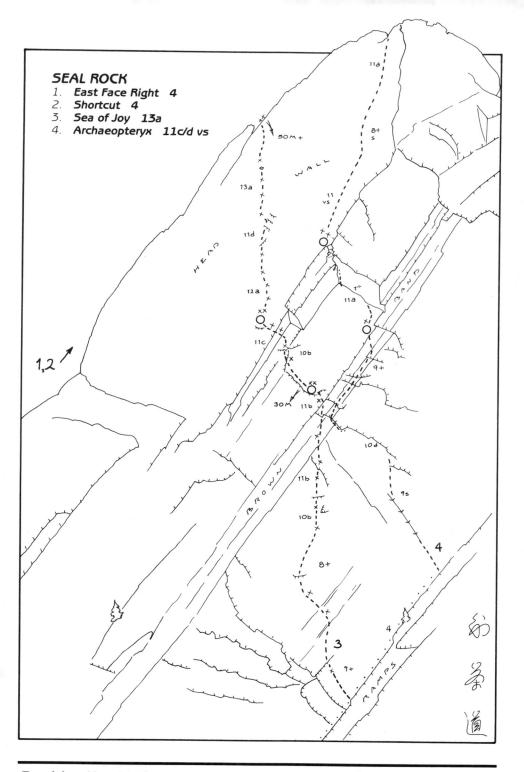

SEAL ROCK
1. East Face Right 4
2. Shortcut 4
3. Sea of Joy 13a
4. Archaeopteryx 11c/d vs

FERN CANYON

Heavily forested and somewhat clandestine, Fern Canyon is nestled between the southeast slope of the Nebel Horn and the northeast slope of Bear Peak. Its narrow entrance lies between the Southern Goose Egg and the north face of The Slab. Beyond The Slab, no real rock climbing exists on the south side of the canyon – but the north side is another story. Until recently, Fern Canyon was a pretty quiet place, but the summer of 1989 brought with it an explosion of new route activity. There are now about 40 bolted face climbs, and one can spend a pleasant day roaming from one route to another in a very beautiful setting. Please use footpaths and trails where they have been established.

The north side of Fern Canyon is characterized by two parallel rock strata that rise to the northwest and culminate at the summit of the Nebel Horn. The northeast faces of both strata are rather low angled, with the southwest faces vertical or overhanging. The more westerly stratum is called the Nebel Horn Ridge, the more easterly, the East Ridge. Other features include a large block along the trail at the bottom of the Nebel Horn Ridge (with the route Superfresh) and Mentor, a pocketed outcrop near the top of the trail.

THE EAST RIDGE

This is the inner sanctuary. The eastern stratum begins in the trees to the north of the Fern Canyon Trail, about 200 yards west of the narrow entrance to the canyon. It then climbs some 1,500 feet to terminate at a minor crest just north of the summit of the Nebel Horn. It consists of two long sections divided by a deep notch. Routes along the southwest face are described from right to left as one would likely hike along the base of the ridge. Approach by hiking the Fern Canyon Trail about 150 feet past the huge, square boulder (Superfresh) that rises on the right. Turn right just before the terminus of the Nebel Horn Ridge and follow a path into the gully between it and the East Ridge.

1. **Castles Made of Sand   11d/12a**
   This route is located on the smooth right wall of a huge dihedral about 200 feet northeast of Superfresh. Follow a line of bolts up the wall near the arete. 65 feet to a bolt anchor.

2. **A Shadow Sickness   9**
   Climb directly up the huge left-facing corner and belay under a roof. Take the crack on the right past a small tree. The crack and corner that branches to the left is rated 10c.

3. **Stemadilemma   11c/d**
   Climb the short, steep, right-facing dihedral about 100 feet left from Castles Made of Sand. Rack up to a #2 Friend.

4. **Chains of Love   12b/c**
   A fantastic roof. Begin about 300 feet up the gully from Castles Made of Sand. Climb a crack up to a good ledge, then master the huge roof. Rack: some mid-range pieces for the first pitch and 6 QDs.

The following three routes are located on the flat west face of the gap, in the middle of the ridge. Begin in a cave formed by a huge boulder that leans against the face. Topo on page 72.

5. **Irish Spring   9**
   Move up and clip an old bolt, then climb the right edge of the face.

6. **Lucky Charms   10d**
   Also known as Rip This Joint. Climb straight up past a bolt to a shallow hole, then move up and right (crux) to gain a short crack. Rack up to one inch.

7. **Leprechaun Promenade   10b**
Also known as Left Joint. This is the leftmost of the three lines. Three bolts. A
second pitch takes the face to the left (7) or the roof at a left-facing flake (10c). Rack
up to a #2 Friend; QDs only for first pitch.

The following routes are on the upper section of the East Ridge.

8. **Exile   12a**
Locate a line of bolts on the left wall of the gap in the ridge, about 75 feet to the
right of Flourescent Grey. Rack: 7 QDs and a 0.5 Tricam. Topo on page 72.

9. **Flourescent Gray   11c**
Begin at the left (northwest) side of the notch. Climb a crack and the right side of a
steep, zigzag arete past several bolts. 85 feet. Rack: 8 QDs and nuts up to one inch.

10. **Everpresent Lane   10d**
About 60 feet left of the gap in the ridge, climb a shallow, right-facing dihedral with
a fixed pin.

The Stealth Slab.

Up to the left of Everpresent Lane is a smooth slab with the following three bolt routes.
Begin from a ledge about 20 feet above the talus. Topo on page 74.

11. **Edgemaster   10d**
Follow a line of bolts up the right side of the slab. Rack: 9 QDs.

12. **Slabmaster   12a**
Follow the middle line of bolts up the slab. Rack: 8 QDs.

13. **Ilga Grimpeur   11b/c**
Follow the left line of bolts along a water streak. Rack: 7 QDs.

About 200 feet up the gully from The Stealth Slab, the ridge forms a series of dihedrals
and aretes that present a good collection of moderate routes.

14. **Superguide   9**
Begin just left of a fallen, dead tree and climb the farthest right of the obvious aretes.
Rappel 80 feet.

15. **Iron Cross   11a**
Climb a left-right-left, flip-flop dihedral past a pin to a belay at two rings. Move left
and chase bolts up the steep face. Rack: mid-sized wires, mid-sized Friends and 7
QDs.

16. **Lightning Bolt Arete   11b**
Begin just left of a bow-shaped tree. Climb a short, left-facing dihedral past a pin
and move left to belay on a ledge with two rings. Follow bolts up the arete. Rack
from a half inch to a #3 Friend, plus 6 QDs.

17. **Haywire   9+**
Begin to the left of the rings on Lightning Bolt Arete. Climb an easy left-facing
corner to a ledge, angle up and right, pass a roof at a slot, and finish with the corner
above.

18. **The Knack   6**
Begin as for Haywire but continue straight up the left-facing dihedral system to the
top of the ridge.

19. **Fountain of Youth   10b**
Climb two-thirds of the Knack, then break out to the right and climb the arete past
three bolts.

Fern Canyon Ridges from the south

4. **The Violator** 13c
5. **Ruby Slipper** 11c s
6. **Rainbow Bridge** 10a

5. **Irish Spring** 9
10. **Everpresent Lane** 10d
12. **Slabmaster** 12a
19. **Fountain of Youth** 10b

EAST RIDGE

THE GOOSE

GAP

15

13

9

5

4

2

NEBEL HORN RIDGE

4

3

1

Fern Canyon Ridges from the south

1. **Castles Made of Sand   11d/12a**
3. **Stemadilemma   11c/d**
4. **Chains of Love   12b/c**
5. **Irish Spring   9**

9. **Flourescent Gray   11c**
13. **Ilga Grimpeur   11b/c**
15. **Iron Cross   11a**

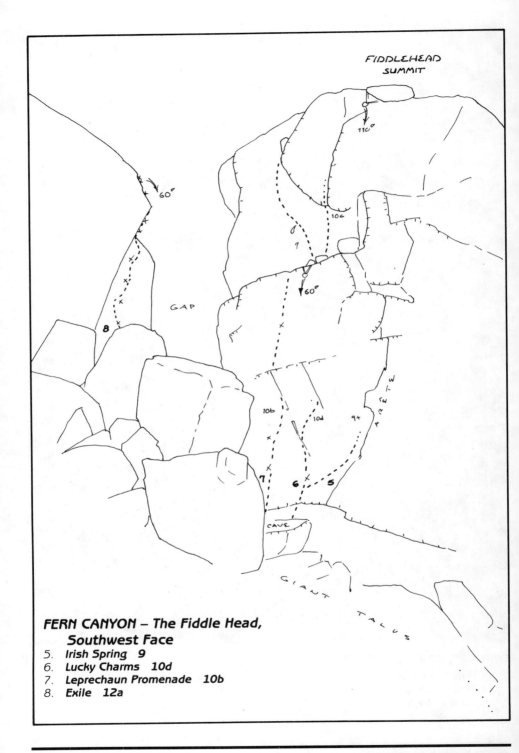

FERN CANYON – The Fiddle Head,
Southwest Face
5. Irish Spring   9
6. Lucky Charms   10d
7. Leprechaun Promenade   10b
8. Exile   12a

Kathy Miller on Edgemaster

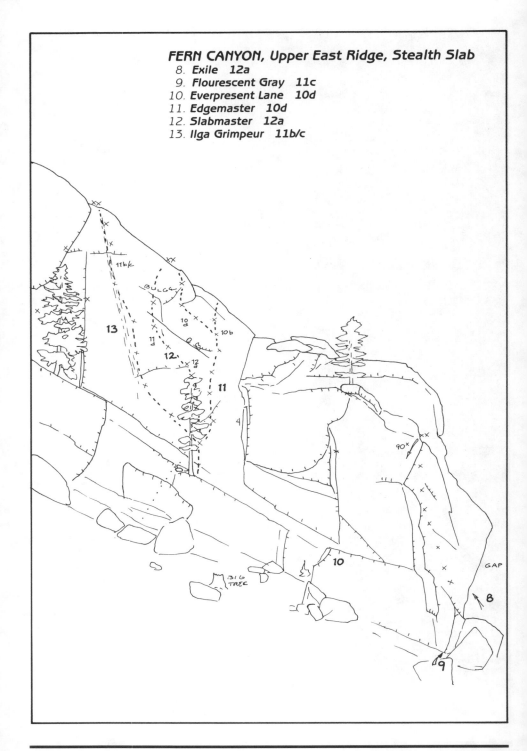

FERN CANYON, Upper East Ridge, Stealth Slab
8. Exile   12a
9. Flourescent Gray   11c
10. Everpresent Lane   10d
11. Edgemaster   10d
12. Slabmaster   12a
13. Ilga Grimpeur   11b/c

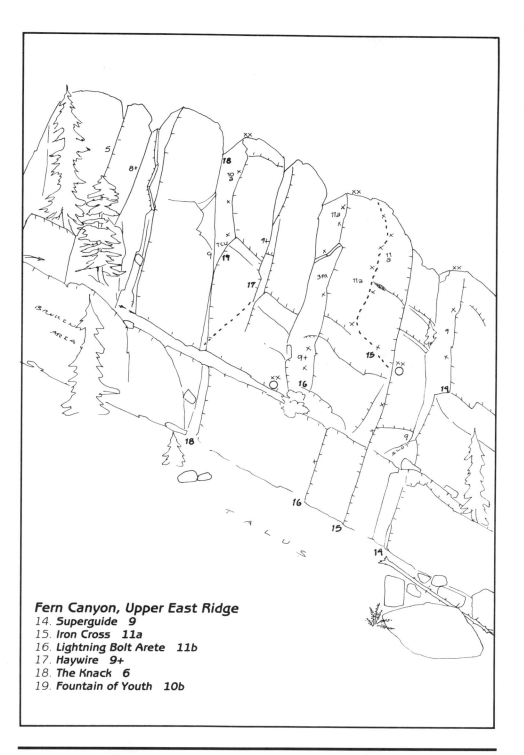

Fern Canyon, Upper East Ridge
14. **Superguide** 9
15. **Iron Cross** 11a
16. **Lightning Bolt Arete** 11b
17. **Haywire** 9+
18. **The Knack** 6
19. **Fountain of Youth** 10b

NEBEL HORN RIDGE

The Nebel Horn Ridge begins just west of Superfresh and culminates as the summit of the Nebel Horn. It consists of three distinct sections separated by gaps or notches, the lower two of which are large flatiron-like formations with good east face routes. These are called Pellaea and Onoclea in ascending order. The third, upper section of the ridge has several good climbs on its steep southwest face and gives rise to the "horn."

Approach the east side of this ridge as for the East Ridge (above). To reach the upper west face, hike farther up the trail to the first northward switchback above an overhanging, pocketed wall with the route Mentor. Head north (right) on a faint path, go through a small notch, and enter the rocky, wooded gully that runs beneath the face. These upper routes also may be reached by hiking north from the col at the top of Fern Canyon. Stay on the west (left) side of the crest until 100 feet beyond the Mars Block, a 60-foot high outcrop with three good bolt routes: 11a, 12c and 12d, right to left. Then, scramble back up to the right to reach the crest and the top of the Nebel Horn Ridge.

Superfresh 12c/d

Climb the obvious, overhanging arete on the large square boulder at the immediate north side of the trail, just before the low point of Pellaea. 5 bolts.

Mentor 12b

This route is on an isolated outcrop about 150 yards past Superfresh just right of the trail. Climb the obvious, overhanging, pocketed wall past four bolts.

The following routes are found along the upper southwest face of the Nebel Horn Ridge. The first two routes begin in a deep cleft capped by a chockstone, about 150 feet past the summit of Onoclea and to the north of Mentor.

1. **Rads for Rookies 8**
   Climb the clean right wall of the cleft past four bolts. Rack: 4 QDs.

2. **False Gods, Real Men 10b/c**
   Climb the steep wall across from Rads. Rack: 6 QDs.

3. **Shot 10c**
   Immediately left of the notch above Onoclea is a smooth, green wall capped by a red wall with overhangs. This route presumably takes the clean, left-facing corner near the right side of the wall and the crack above.

4. **The Violator 13c**
   Begin a short way left of Shot. 1. Climb the slab past several bolts up to the base of an overhanging arete (10b). 2. Climb the arete. Rack: QDs.

5. **Ruby Slipper 11c s**
   Begin up on a ledge about midway between the cleft with the chockstone and the top of the ridge. Climb a thin crack up a conspicuous red slab. Rack up to one inch.

6. **Rainbow Bridge 10a**
   At the top of the ridge, directly below the summit of the Nebel Horn, a clean buttress leans out to the south. Scramble up a short slab and belay behind a tree. Climb the overhang (crux) and the face above, near to the arete. Four bolts.

The route Superfresh, along the Fern Canyon Trail

THE SLAB

The Slab is a big piece of rock – probably the largest of the Flatirons. It is the southern guardian to the narrows of Fern Canyon. Among its unique features is that it is wide instead of tall. The east face of the Slab is about 500 feet high and 2000 feet long and offers unlimited creativity to the adventurous slab monger. The northwest face is vertical to overhanging, and has given rise to several high-quality bolted face routes. To reach The Slab, hike the north branch of the Shanahan Trail until directly below the east face – you can't miss it. To reach the north and west faces, continue north to a junction with the Fern Canyon Trail. Hike up through the narrows of Fern Canyon and pick up a footpath that breaks off to the south at some large boulders.

1. **Northeast Arete 5**

   This is a good Flatiron route up the north margin of the east face. Go under the hanging flake.

2. **Just Another Boy's Climb 11d**

   This is the furthest left of the bolt routes on the north face. Climb a slab to a stance and belay (8). Climb jugs up a water streak, make a move to the left, then a strenuous hand traverse out under the roof. Heelhook and crank up to an anchor. Rappel 100 feet. Rack: 8 QDs and mid-range Friends.

3. **Boys with Power Toys 12b**

   This steep and strenuous line powers up through the massive, stepped overhang about 50 feet to the right from Boy's Climb. Look for a line of bolts. 70 feet. Rack: 9 QDs.

4. **Whipping Post 11d**

   Begin up to the right of Power Toys, where the roof fades out. Climb up and hand traverse left, up past a ring bolt (crux), then up fine rock (9) toward the crest. Rappel 90 feet. Rack: 8 QDs.

5. **Undertow 12b**

   "Jug dyno paradise." About 100 feet south of Whipping Post, follow a line of bolts up the awe-inspiring, overhanging wall. 80 feet. Rack: 7 QDs and a #3 Friend.

FERN CANYON

THE SLAB
1. Northeast Arete 5
2. Just Another Boy's Climb   11d
3. Boys with Power Toys   12b
4. Whipping Post   11d
5. Undertow   12b

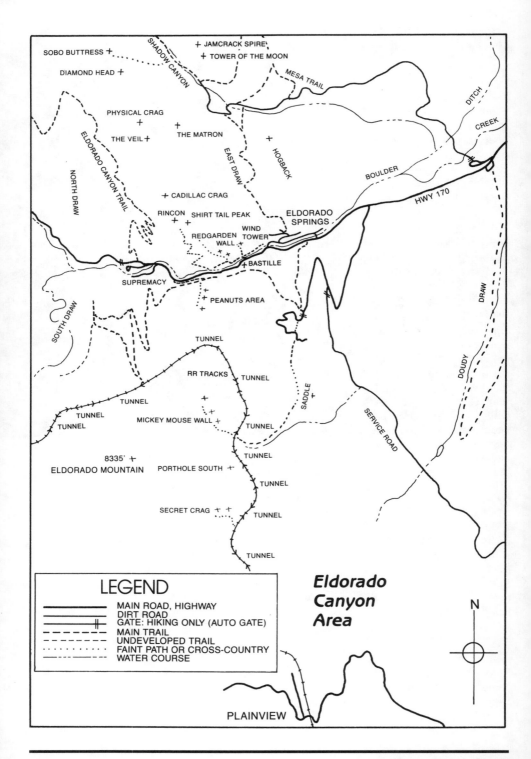

Eldorado
Canyon
Area

N

Eldorado Canyon ───────────

IN THE WORLD OF ROCK CLIMBING there are a few places that require no introduction. Eldorado Canyon is one of them. Since the middle of the century it has been the central arena and seat of power for Colorado climbing and has given rise to some of the finest and most difficult routes in North America. On any fair day there are climbers in the canyon, but during the summer, Eldorado can look like a Grateful Dead concert at Red Rocks – well, almost. Popular routes such as the Bastille Crack will sometimes have a climbing party on each pitch, and, as in Yosemite, waiting in line to begin a route is not uncommon. Yet, at times, in the off season, one might find himself alone in the canyon – an awesome experience. The Indians knew Eldorado as a place of great power, and indeed it is. Come and meet the spirit of the canyon. If you haven't climbed on Red Garden Wall, the Bastille, or Rincon, you haven't been cragging in Colorado.

Eldorado features the beautiful, polychromed rock of the Fountain Formation, awe-inspiring verticality, more than 500 routes ranging in difficulty from 0 to 13c, ludicrously easy access and the almost claustrophobic proximity of the some of the most famous crags in America. Yet, true scenic solitude awaits those who visit the more outlying features, such as Peanuts, Rincon, or Cadillac Crag.

Information, books, maps, T-shirts and an indoor climbing demonstration (!) are available at the Visitor Center at the west end of the park. Also at the west end is a delightful and popular picnic area featuring a babbling brook and graffiti-proof tables. Gasoline, groceries, beverages, and the like are not avilable at the state park. The nearest facilities are three miles east at the junction of Highways 170 and 93. Find here Dyno-mart with gas, groceries, and a telephone, Fiesta Liquor, and an Ethiopian restaurant called Ras Casas. The Eldorado Springs Resort, along with swimming, sells some food, perhaps beer, and excellent artesian water. The International Alpine School is immediately northwest of the pool and offers climbing instruction and equipment (sales and rental). The tiny town of Eldorado Springs has a post office and a horse concession but offers no other public services. Nearby Boulder – chic, new age, a place to be – offers every conceivable facility and amenity.

How to get there:

Eldorado Canyon lies between Boulder Mountain on the north and Eldorado Mountain on the south and is cut deeply by South Boulder Creek. To reach the canyon from Boulder, drive south on Broadway, which becomes Highway 93 beyond the Table Mesa area. Continue south for a few more miles and turn west on Highway 170 (Eldorado Springs Drive). After three miles, enter the town of Eldorado Springs; another quarter mile brings one to the entrance to Eldorado Canyon State Park. Coming from Denver, head north on Interstate 25, northwest on the Boulder-Denver Turnpike (Highway 36), and west on Highway 170 (take the Louisville-Eldorado exit, up and over the turnpike – right on 170). See map on pages 82 and 83.

Remember that most of the crags described in this chapter are within the boundary of Eldorado Canyon State Park. This means that you will be a "park visitor" when you come here to climb, and that you will be subject to the rules and regulations of the park. Don't forget to pick up a park pass.

───────────────────────────────

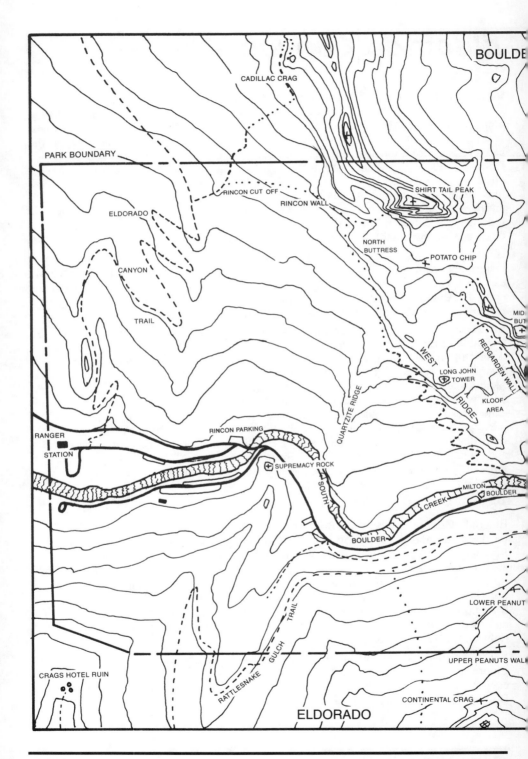

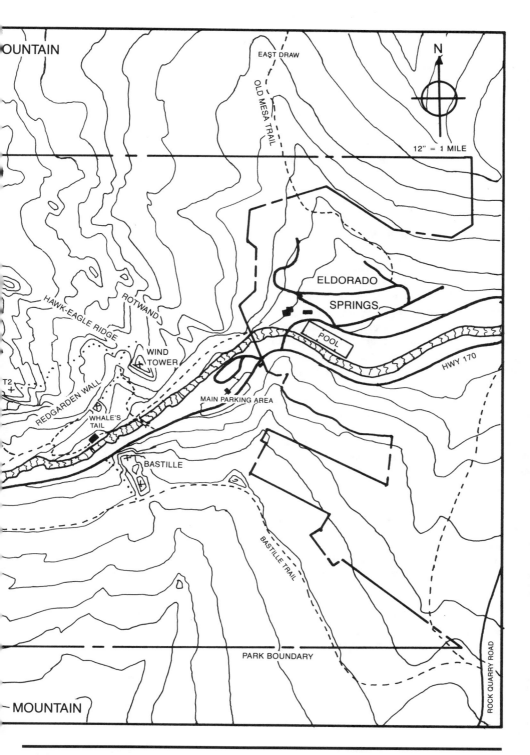

TRAILS

Though none of the trails that begin in Eldorado Canyon State Park connect coherently with other trail systems, three fine routes exist, all of which are useful in reaching outlying crags. Several less-developed trails, typically in pathetic disrepair, wind along the bases of the park's major crags and serve as routes of approach and descent. These paths, such as the one along the west side of the Bastille, are more dangerous than most of the climbs to which they lead.

The Streambank Trail begins at the footbridge that crosses South Boulder Creek just east of the Bastille, and parallels the north side of the stream to the east and west. To the west, the trail comes to an abrupt dead end where the south buttress of the West Ridge drops into the creek. A short scramble over this obstacle leads to the newly-built West Ridge Trail.

The Wind Tower Trail begins at the north side of the footbridge and zigzags up the talus gully between the Wind Tower and the Whale's Tail.

The Red Garden Wall – West Face Trail breaks off to the north from the Streambank Trail just beyond Pickpocket Wall and climbs along the southwest face of Red Garden Wall. This trail, which leads to many important routes, is in terrible shape and has severe erosion problems. Please be careful and stay close to the wall.

The West Ridge Trail begins about 100 feet beyond the west end of the Streambank Trail and climbs the steep slope beneath the southwest face of the West Ridge. One must ford South Boulder Creek or climb over the bottom of the West Ridge to reach it. This trail was developed recently by volunteers and is in good condition.

The Bastille Trail – now apparently named the **Fowler Trail** – begins on the left (south) side of the road about 0.3 mile west of the Bastille and shares its first 100 yards or so with the Rattlesnake Gulch Trail. After heading east for about 200 yards, the trail is obliterated by a 100-foot-wide rock slide – a dangerous crossing. Once east of the slide, the path passes through a notch that was blasted in the back of the Bastille, then curves around into a brushy draw and eventually intersects a wide dirt road that leads to an active rock quarry in the east face of Eldorado Mountain. Just before this intersection, another trail heads down the gulch to the north and comes out near the post office in Eldorado Springs. This is not within the current boundaries of the state park. One may use either one of these trails to begin the walk to Mickey Mouse Wall.

The Rattlesnake Gulch Trail begins as for the Bastille Trail but breaks off to the southwest after about 100 yards. It winds along a draw in beautiful wooded terrain with compelling views of Red Garden Wall and the West Ridge. After about a mile, a grassy terrace opens up on the north that bears the ruins of the Crags Resort, a hotel complex that burned to the ground circa 1911. At this point, the trail bifurcates to the south and west. The south branch climbs up to the Denver and Rio Grande railroad grade that winds around the east and north slopes of Eldorado Mountain. The west branch climbs gently around to the northwest, passes a junction on the left, and leads out to a scenic overlook on the north ridge of Eldorado Mountain. The trail that proceeds from the junction 50 yards south of the overlook cuts back to the south and southeast and after about a half mile, joins the trail that leads up to the railroad grade.

The Eldorado Canyon Trail begins near the west boundary of the state park. It climbs northwest through rugged, primitive terrain and reaches Walker Ranch (Boulder County open space) in about 4 miles. To find the beginning to this superb trail, walk about 50 yards west on the road from the small "Rincon parking area," just north of Supremacy, and find the trail on the right (north). This point also may be reached by picking up a short connecting trail just east of the Visitor Center that leads up to the road.

The Rincon Cut-Off leads to Rincon Wall, Shirt Tail Peak, the upper West Ridge, and Cadillac Crag. Begin on the Eldorado Canyon Trail. Within the first half mile, the trail contours around a draw and heads southeast onto a sparsely wooded ridge. About 150 feet beyond the third switchback on this ridge, the trail begins to descend. At the high point, a footpath goes straight up the grassy slope on the right (east) and leads up to the broad talus field below Rincon Wall. A left branch, just before the talus field, leads northeast through a stand of trees to the long talus field below Cadillac Crag.

THE WIND TOWER

The narrow pyramid of the Wind Tower rises 300 feet directly above the north shore of South Boulder Creek and is host to several of the most popular routes in Colorado. It is difficult to estimate how many hundreds or thousands of people make ascents of Wind Ridge, Tagger and Calypso each year, but the fact that these routes seldom are unoccupied stimulates the imagination. Nearly all of the routes on the Wind Tower lie along the south and west faces and are up to three pitches in length. The routes on the south face are, with some exception, more difficult and poorly protected. On the west face, the routes are lower-angled and better protected, but there is loose rock, especially near the summit, and one should be reluctant to climb beneath another party.

To reach the Wind Tower, take the footbridge across South Boulder Creek where paths branch to the west and south faces of the crag. To descend from the summit, scramble north along the ridge for about 100 feet to a U-shaped notch with a rappel anchor. Make a short rappel or downclimb (4) to the steep and loose slope below. There is a long, rotten ledge system two pitches up that traverses the entire west face. This is exposed and dangerous in places but allows for a walk-off from all routes including those on the south face. A better escape from the top of the south face routes, however, is to downclimb either of two easy grooves on the west face to the top of a huge, leaning boulder, then reverse the first few moves of Calypso.

The following two routes begin from a pedestal at the top of a ramp that angles up and left toward the middle of the south face (2).

1. **Scotch and Soda   11b/c s**
   A testpiece of the 1970s. Climb up through the roof above the pedestal (crux) and proceed as shown in the topo.
2. **The Yellow Traverse   9 vs**
   A good direct start to Metamorphosis. From the pedestal, drop down a bit on the west side, then work up and left. Rack: a #4 RP.

Approach the following two routes via the Yellow Traverse, King's X, or one of the easy grooves on the west face.

3. **Metamorphosis   9+ s**
   A classic face climb. Begin from a belay just above a small vine maple tree at the low (east) end of a ramp above King's X. A variation called Ur-ine Trouble (10b/c s) moves left and climbs a right-leaning, right-facing dihedral near the top of the pitch.
4. **Disguise   10b s**
   Just another adrenalin rush. Begin in a slot down and right from the left edge of the south face. Rack up to a #2 Friend and don't plan on using much of it.

5. **Rainbow Wall   13a**
   Scramble about a third of the way up a left-facing dihedral and belay. Undercling out to the left (9, #2 Friend), stretch up to clip the first bolt, and follow a line of bolts up and left to easier ground. Rack: a #2 Friend and 6 QDs.

6. **King's X   11a s/vs**
   This was a wild ride a decade ago when most of the original fixed pro still was in place. Now, only a couple of pins remain and the route has become quite serious. Begin just right of an arched roof at the bottom of the south face.

WIND TOWER – West Face

7. **Calypso   6**
   A sea nymph who, for seven years, detained Odysseus on the island of Ogygia. Also a wildflower, a form of music from the West Indies – and a superb route. Begin just left of the huge boulder that leans against the wall. Calypso Direct (8) climbs the left side of the roof to the ledge with a pine tree on Tagger.

8. **Reggae   8**
   From the bolt anchor on Calypso, move down and right about 10 feet, then jam and stem up a large, right-facing dihedral. The crux is a finger crack at the top (wired stoppers). Belay *a cheval* on the natural bridge. Rack up to a #2 Friend.

9. **Tagger   10b/c s**
   This very popular route has been the scene of some serious accidents. The first pitch – now missing a traditional fixed pin – is tricky to protect, and the roof of the upper pitch relies on a couple of very old pitons.

10. **Wind Ridge   6 or 8**
    This famous passage takes the skyline ridge as seen from the footbridge, and possibly is the most frequently-climbed route in Colorado. From the huge block that leans against the face, hike up around the lower buttress of Wind Ridge and cut back south onto a ledge with a Douglas fir tree. Begin with a left-leaning ramp (6) or a steep crack to the right (8). One may exit at the walk-off ledge or climb a final pitch to the summit.

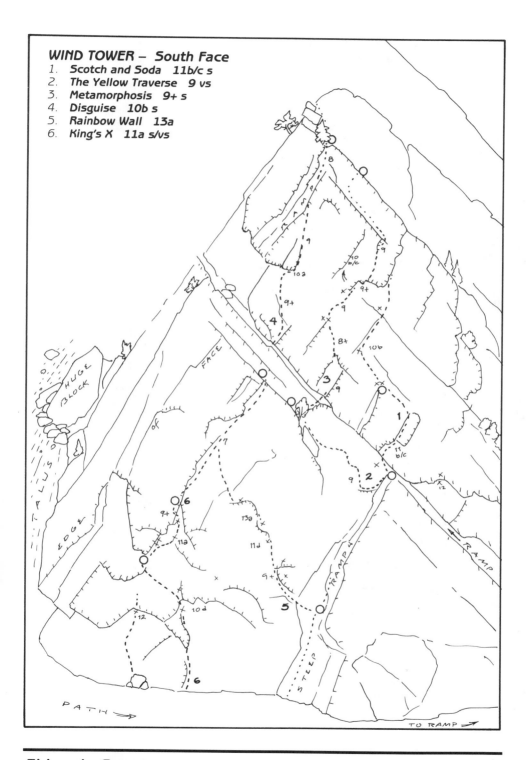

WIND TOWER – South Face
1. Scotch and Soda   11b/c s
2. The Yellow Traverse   9 vs
3. Metamorphosis   9+ s
4. Disguise   10b s
5. Rainbow Wall   13a
6. King's X   11a s/vs

WIND TOWER
2. **The Yellow Traverse 9 vs**
3. **Metamorphosis 9+ s**
6. **King's X 11a s/vs**
7. **Calypso 6**
8. **Reggae 8**
9. **Tagger 10b/c s**
10. **Wind Ridge 6 or 8**

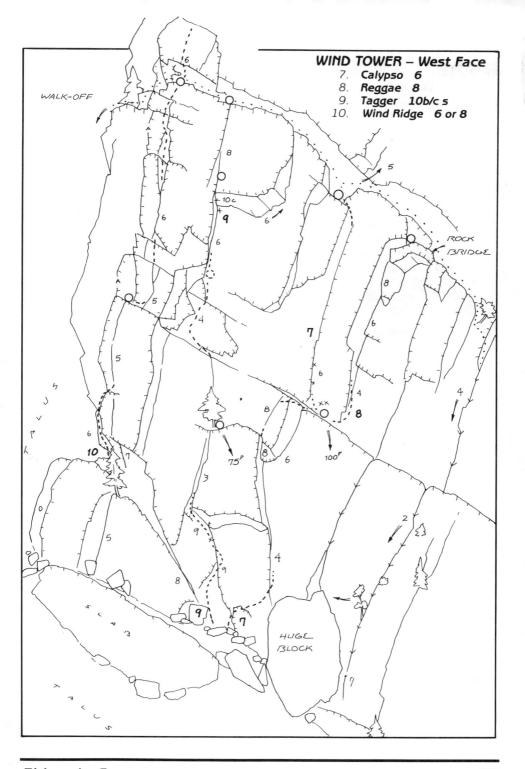

WIND TOWER – West Face
7. **Calypso 6**
8. **Reggae 8**
9. **Tagger 10b/c s**
10. **Wind Ridge 6 or 8**

WALK-OFF

ROCK BRIDGE

HUGE BLOCK

THE WHALE'S TAIL

The Whale's Tail is the 100-foot-high, curvilinear tower directly across South Boulder Creek from the Bastille. It is recognized easily by a large cave at the bottom of its south face. The crag features numerous boulder problems and short routes that see a good deal of traffic – not so much because they are great routes, but because of their ready access. The upper west face, however, has a couple of the best easy crack climbs in Eldorado.

South Face

1. **Horangutan   12a**
   Begin just right of the cave. Climb overhanging jugs to an apex, left along a crack with pins, then straight up a short crack to a bolt anchor.

2. **Monument Direct   13a**
   This bizarre route begins back inside the cave and follows a line of bolts out the roof to join Horangutan. Here, one competes with pigeons and bats for air space. It was toproped a zillion times and eventually led free in 1980 by a person whose name seems to have gotten lost.

3. **N.E.D.   12a**
   This is a popular toprope problem just west of the cave. Due to scanty pro, it has not caught on as a lead.

West Face

To reach the following routes, take the Streambank Trail to the cement slab southwest of the Whale's Tail, then hike up the talus gully to the northeast.

4. **West Dihedral   4   e**
   Begin from a big ledge about 50 feet up on the west face. Climb the big, left-facing dihedral at the right. Rack up to a #4 Friend.

5. **West Crack   2   e**
   From the big ledge, work up through a bulge and jam a good crack (with lots of face holds) to a belay alcove near the summit. A practice belay also may be set in a hole about half-way up.

6. **Jack the Ripper   9+ s**
   An Eldorado mini-classic. Begin on a ledge at the base of a huge, left-facing dihedral at the north side of the west face. Climb the slab that forms the left side of the dihedral up to the big roof (8 s), then hand traverse right across the right wall to the arete (9+).

7. **C'est What?   11b**
   Follow a line of bolts on the right wall of the dihedral of Jack the Ripper. Rack: RPs, stoppers, and a #2 Friend. This is a good pitch.

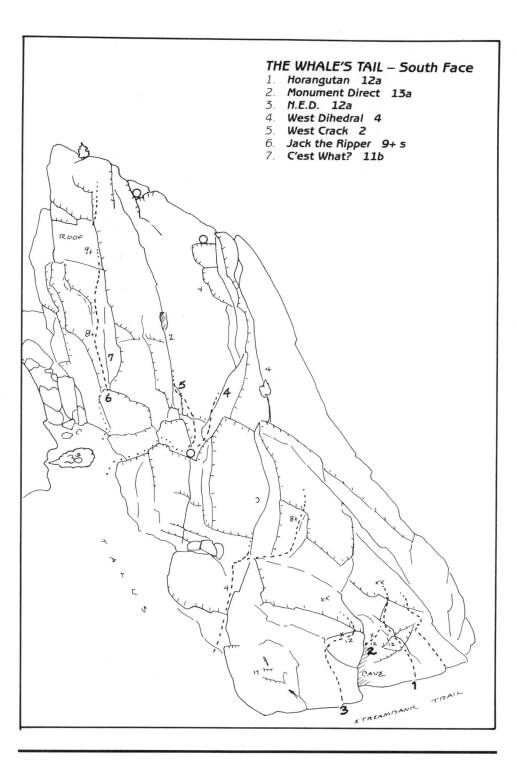

THE WHALE'S TAIL – South Face
1. Horangutan 12a
2. Monument Direct 13a
3. N.E.D. 12a
4. West Dihedral 4
5. West Crack 2
6. Jack the Ripper 9+ s
7. C'est What? 11b

Christian Griffith on Lakme, Red Garden Wall

photo: Dan Hare

RED GARDEN WALL

As one approaches Eldorado Canyon from the east, the view is dominated by the serrated skyline of Red Garden Wall as it climbs northward. Here, amid sheer towers and outlandish aretes, lie some of the most aesthetic, difficult, unusual, and sought-after climbs in North America. Red Garden Wall is the largest crag in the Boulder area and has far more routes than any other continuous feature. It is also the highest crag, with some routes having seven and eight pitches.

Approaches. To reach the southeast face (the Bulge Wall), take the footbridge across South Boulder Creek and hike up the Wind Tower Trail until it is obvious to cut left beneath the face. To reach the South Buttress and southwest face, hike the Streambank Trail past the Whale's Tail to a big cement slab and scramble up the talus to the base of the wall. To reach the west face, continue west along the Streambank Trail to where it climbs up above the creek and passes a small rib that overhangs to the west (Pickpocket Buttress). A primitive trail wanders up along the west side of this buttress all the way to the west face area. A sign at the cutoff reads, "West Face Trail."

Descents. There are several ways to descend from the upper reaches of Red Garden Wall. The best one to use depends upon which route has been completed.

East Slab Descent Route is by far the easiest way to escape from the summits of Lumpe Tower, Tower One, Tower Two and the South Buttress. From Tower One or Lumpe Tower, scramble down to the notch between the two and work southeast down a gully to the saddle between Towers One and Two. From here, scramble a short way into the wooded gully just east of Tower Two, then hike down to the southeast about 150 feet to where the gully drops off and it is easy to get up onto the rib on the left (northeast). Scramble down this rib (the upper South Buttress) to the south about 150 feet, cut back to the northeast, climb down (or around) a short overhang, and scoot down a deep groove for about 100 feet. Stem down past a bulge, go left into another groove, descend about 100 feet, and go down to the right (southeast) to a large, grassy ledge with some juniper trees. From here, go left into a V-slot, and downclimb to the gully between the East Slabs and Hawkeagle Ridge. Follow a primitive footpath down the brushy gully, walk beneath Cinch Crack, climb down around either side of a giant chockstone (the east side if wet), and on to the Wind Tower Trail. NOTE: if you are not familiar with this descent, do not try to do it in the dark.

Dirty Deed Rappel. If, for example, you left gear at the bottom of a west-side route, such as the Yellow Spur, it is possible to descend the gully to the WEST from the notch between Tower One and Lumpe Tower. Make two long rappels west from the notch to the Red Ledge, which runs across the west face, and scramble north to a tree with slings above the West Chimney. Rappel 150 feet west to the talus.

Naked Edge Rappel. To descend from the Upper Ramp, downclimb to its low, south end. BE VERY CAREFUL OF LOOSE ROCK. Climb up and around a little buttress, and find a bolt anchor on the east-sloping platform beneath the first pitch of the Naked Edge. Rappel 75 feet to the southeast and find another bolt anchor hidden behind a south-facing block. Rappel 150 feet southwest to the ground, or make two half-rope rappels using an intermediate anchor.

Pigeon Crack Rappel. It also is possible to descend from the top of the Upper Ramp by rappelling 150 feet WEST down the Pigeon Crack. The beginning of this descent is identified by slings around a spike of rock a couple of yards down to the west from the top of the ramp, at its NORTH side.

To descend from the summit ridge of the Middle Buttress – that is, from such routes as Rewritten and Green Slab Direct – scramble north about 400 feet along the east side of the ridge crest to a notch. Beyond the notch, the terrain climbs up toward Shirt Tail Peak. To the west, a navigable gully descends to the main draw between Red Garden Wall and the West Ridge. Descend the loose gully, then follow the base of the wall back down toward South Boulder Creek. Be very careful of loose rock, and stay next to the cliff as much as possible.

The routes are listed from right to left, beginning with the Bulge Wall (southeast face). Bear in mind that there are dozens of routes on Red Garden Wall not described in this book. See *Boulder Climbs South* for a complete representation.

RED GARDEN WALL – The Bulge Wall

The Bulge Wall is the steep, blackened face immediately behind the Whale's Tail; it is actually the lower southeast face of the south buttress. To escape from the top of the Bulge, Blackwalk and the like, traverse around to the north and intersect the East Slab Descent Route.

1. **The Bulge   7 s or 9 s**
   This classic tour has reasonable pro at all the hard spots, but because the second and third pitches zigzag back and forth, it is not well-suited to beginner seconds. The leader should be good at route-finding and be prepared to "dice it up" a bit on the easier sections. Begin at the far east end of the grassy bench above the Whale's Tail. Four good pitches.

2. **Backtalk   10c s**
   A fine face pitch with less-than-great bolt work for a rap-route. Begin as for Blackwalk, but break off to the right on the initial leftward traverse. Rack: a #1.5 or 2 Friend and 4 QDs.

3. **Blackwalk   10b/c s**
   Classic. Begin near the middle of the grassy platform behind the Whale's Tail. Rack up to a #2 Friend, but only a #2 Friend and a few QDs are of any use on the first pitch.

4. **Back in Black   11c**
   This is a fairly new route to the left of Blackwalk. Work up and left, then follow a line of six bolts up to a two-bolt anchor and rappel. Rack: 6 QDs.

RED GARDEN WALL – The South Buttress

The South Buttress is the large, rounded buttress that forms the southermost aspect of Red Garden Wall. The following routes begin 150 feet due north of the cement slab (just west of the Whale's Tail).

5. **C'est La Morte   9**
   Begin atop some large blocks that lean against the base of the wall due north of the cement slab. 160 feet; beware of rope drag.

6. **Je T'aime   12c s**
   This very sustained route ascends the beautiful, dark-green slab between C'est La Morte and C'est La Vie. It is seldom led due to the arrangement of the bolts. Begin with C'est La Morte. 100 feet. Rack: a #2 Friend at the undercling (or just solo up to the first bolt) and 4 QDs.

Red Garden Wall from the southeast showing the East Slab Descent Route.

1. *The Bulge   7 s or 9 s*
3. *Blackwalk   10b/c s*
7. *C'est La Vie   9 or 11c*
12. *Genesis   11a   or 12c*
18. *The Naked Edge   11a*

7. **C'est La Vie   9 or 11c**

An Ament masterpiece. This route ascends the clean face and giant, right-leaning dihedral due north of the cement slab. Begin atop some large blocks that lean up against the base of the wall. Note that there are several variations to this route, all of which are quite good.

8. **Desdichado   13b/c**

This is considered by some to be Christian Griffith's finest route; it also is his most well-protected route. Begin with C'est La Vie and climb the dihedral through the crux (11c). Arc out left along a line of bolts to the arete, then straight up. Rappel 165 feet.

9. **Pansee Sauvage   11b s**

Pronounced pahn say so vaj: mind of the savage. Begin this superb face pitch about midway between C'est La Vie and Genesis. There are three bolts, one at each crux. Finish at the bolt belay on C'est La Vie. 80 feet; commonly toproped. Rack: 3 QDs.

10. **Le Boomerang   11d**

This is an exciting, if brief, connecting pitch between the first 50 feet of Genesis and the two-bolt belay on C'est La Vie.

11. **Lakme   13b**

Another Griffith testpiece with good pro. Begin with Genesis. Five bolts. Rappel 165 feet. Rack: 8 or 9 QDs and a #4 Rock (above the last bolt).

12. **Genesis   11a   or 12c**

Classic. Due north of the cement slab, some large blocks form a ledge along the base of Red Garden Wall. Genesis begins from the highest point to the left. Rack: #2 and 2.5 Friends and 8 QDs. A direct finish called Leviticus (12c), climbs straight out the upper roof via three bolts. Note that the so-called first pitch (11a) ends at a two-bolt anchor 80 feet up and is supremely popular.

13. **Anthill Direct   9 s**

Classic. This is the only route that scales the entire South Buttress. The traditional start ascends a blackwashed ramp just left of Genesis, which is not recommended. A better option is to climb Touch and Go (8+) to the grassy ramp below the upper wall and continue with the regular line. Only the second pitch above Touch and Go is at all runout (6 s).

14. **Redguard   8+ s**

Classic. Be advised that this is a very dangerous route and has claimed more victims than any other on Red Garden Wall. The line is subject to rockfall and has long, unprotected sections. The first pitch (the crux), which was originally protected by fixed pins, is the most hazardous because none of the pins remain and nut placements are tricky. This has been the scene of a despairing number of ground falls. Redguard is not a good route for a novice leader. Begin at a small clearing about 75 feet west of Genesis. From the top of the route, scramble east over the shoulder of the South Buttress to join the East Slab Descent Route.

15. **The Contest   11d**

Begin just left of Redguard. Follow a line of bolts up and left around the arete. Rack: 5 QDs.

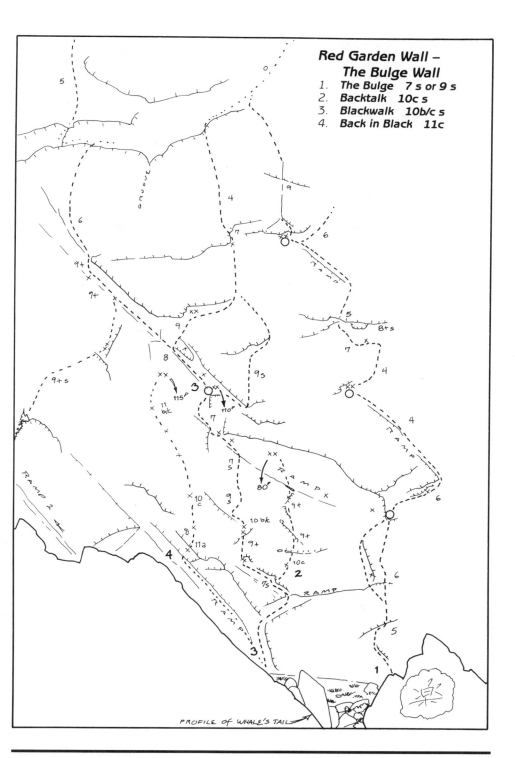

Red Garden Wall –
The Bulge Wall
1. The Bulge   7 s or 9 s
2. Backtalk   10c s
3. Blackwalk   10b/c s
4. Back in Black   11c

PROFILE OF WHALE'S TAIL

RED GARDEN WALL – Tower Two
6. Je T'aime 12c s
7. C'est La Vie 9 or 11c
12. Genesis 11a or 12c

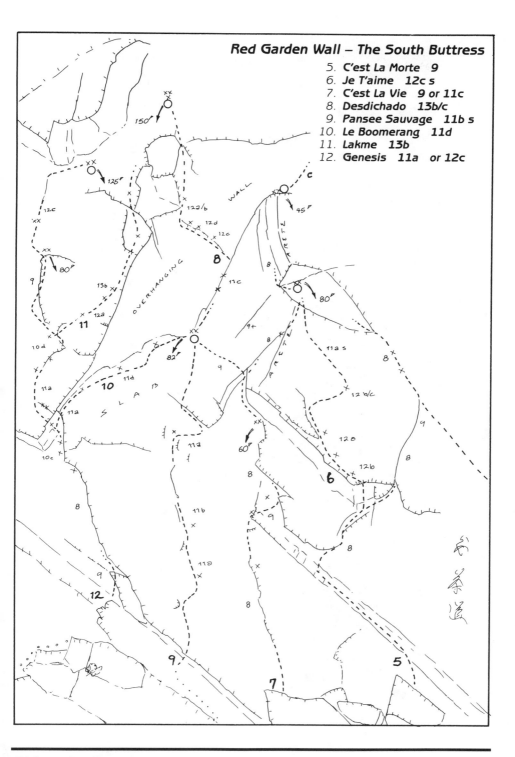

5. *C'est La Morte* **9**
6. *Je T'aime* **12c s**
7. *C'est La Vie* **9 or 11c**
8. *Desdichado* **13b/c**
9. *Pansee Sauvage* **11b s**
10. *Le Boomerang* **11d**
11. *Lakme* **13b**
12. *Genesis* **11a or 12c**

Mark Sonnenfeld on Genesis, Red Garden Wall

photo: Bob Rotert

RED GARDEN WALL – Tower Two

Viewed from the road beneath the Bastille, Tower Two forms the sharp arete and summit to the left of the South Buttress.

16. **Centaur   12c**
    A dramatic aid climb from the 1960s – now, only the last pitch is ascended ordinarily. Scramble up the East Slab Descent Route and across a ledge that leads to the east corner of the summit of Tower Two. Rappel 80 feet to a sling belay at the bottom of the overhanging pitch. Some wires and small Friends will be needed as well as about 10 QDs.

17. **Diving Board   11a**
    Classic. This is a spectacular, overhanging crack climb up the center of the northeast face of Tower Two. Begin with Redguard. Rack up to a #4 Friend.

18. **The Naked Edge   11a**
    A legendary climb. From the road in front of the Bastille, this route is seen following the skyline of the narrow south arete of Tower Two. It usually is approached via Touch and Go or a cavernous ramp that angles up and left from the start to Redguard. From the grassy ramp above Touch and Go, work up through the obvious cave and belay from bolts at the base of the first pitch – a beautiful finger crack (11a). The last two pitches are the most difficult. Rack up to a #4 Friend.

19. **Slow Train Comin'   11a**
    Beautiful slab. From the belay above the cave, follow a line of bolts up the slab to the right of the first pitch of the Naked Edge. Rack: 8 QDs.

20. **Genius Loci   11c**
    This steep and dramatic route begins at the base of the Naked Edge. Climb around to the west side of the arete and follow a line of bolts to the top of the second pitch. 150 feet. Rack: 9 QDs.

21. **Wingless Victory   13b**
    Climb the overhanging arete just right of the bombay chimney on the fourth pitch of the Naked Edge. 60 feet, 5 bolts.

22. **The Sickness Unto Death   12b**
    Climb the left side of the overhanging arete on the fifth pitch of the Naked Edge. Rack: 7 QDs and a #3 Friend.

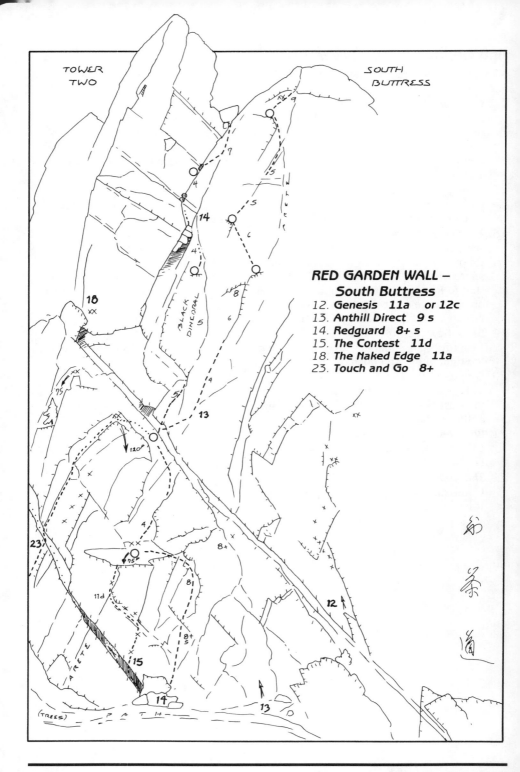

RED GARDEN WALL –
South Buttress
12. **Genesis 11a or 12c**
13. **Anthill Direct 9 s**
14. **Redguard 8+ s**
15. **The Contest 11d**
18. **The Naked Edge 11a**
23. **Touch and Go 8+**

TOWER ONE

LUMPE TOWER
TOWER TWO

UPPER
RAMP

18

SOUTH BUTTRESS

LOWER
RAMP

13

23

7

The South Face of Red Garden Wall from the Bastille Trail

7. *C'est La Vie* *9 or 11c*   18. *The Naked Edge* *11a*
13. *Anthill Direct* *9 s*   23. *Touch and Go* *8+*

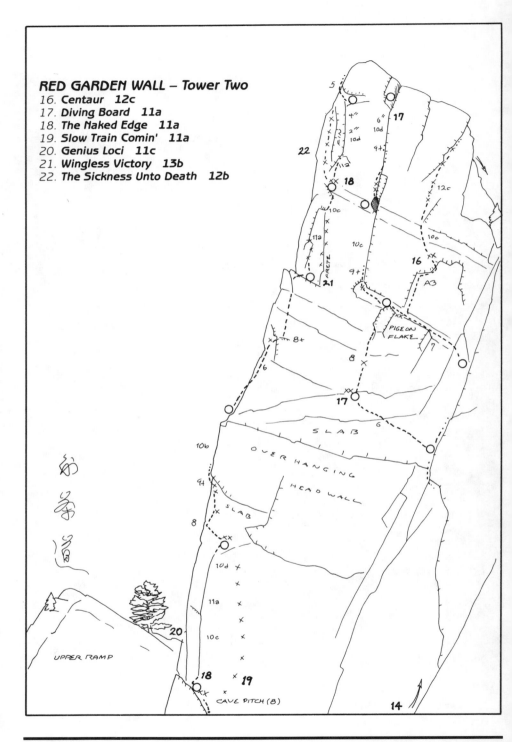

RED GARDEN WALL – Tower Two

16. *Centaur   12c*
17. *Diving Board   11a*
18. *The Naked Edge   11a*
19. *Slow Train Comin'   11a*
20. *Genius Loci   11c*
21. *Wingless Victory   13b*
22. *The Sickness Unto Death   12b*

On the first pitch of the Naked Edge.

RED GARDEN WALL – Southwest Face

The south face of Red Garden Wall ends at an arete at the very base of Tower Two. From here, the wall climbs toward the northwest and forms an immense southwest face that is transected by two broad, diagonal ledges – the Lower Ramp and the Upper Ramp. Approach via the Streambank Trail.

23. Touch and Go 8+

A very popular pitch. Begin about 75 feet up along the southwest face from its low point. Climb up and left through a roof (8+), up through a slot, and up a beautiful, obtuse, right-facing dihedral with the crux near the top. 120 feet. Rack up to a #2 Friend.

24. Bolting for Glory 10a

A popular variation. From the ramp at the top of the first half of Touch and Go, climb straight up past three bolts (crux), then arc up and left past a fourth bolt to join Touch and Go near the top.

25. Scratch and Sniff 11d/12a

Climb the wall just left of Touch and Go past four bolts. Rack: RPs, small wires, QDs.

26. T2 11a s

Classic. The initial overhang originally was rated 9+, but unless you start from a shoulder stand, it is more like 11a. Begin about 60 feet left of Touch and Go beneath a flake and drilled baby angle. Crank up and right from some slanting fingerlocks, heelhook, and head for the pin (crux). This is a bad groundfall if you blow the clip-in. Work up the vertical face and continue as shown in the topo. Seven or eight pitches. Rack up to a #3.5 Friend.

27. Jules Verne 11a s

This long route is one of the classic testpieces of Red Garden Wall. The second pitch above the Upper Ramp involves difficult, intricate moves well above the last good pro. Begin with T2 but work up and left from the lip of the initial roof.

28. Lene's Dream 11b/c s

This is a beautiful, continuously difficult pitch with poor protection. From the Upper Ramp, climb the dihedral and crux headwall of Jules Verne to the rotten band, then climb straight up to the top of the second pitch of the Naked Edge.

Ken Brink hangs it out on the Ruper Traverse

Eldorado Canyon

Red Garden Wall from the southwest

12. **Genesis 11a   or 12c**
14. **Redguard 8+ s**
23. **Touch and Go 8+**

27. **Jules Verne 11a s**
41. **Rosy Crucifixion 10a**
44. **Ruper 8**

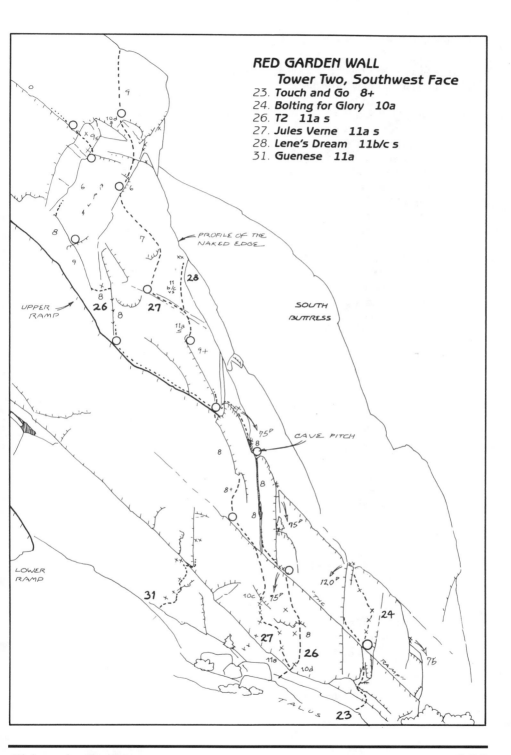

RED GARDEN WALL
Tower Two, Southwest Face
23. Touch and Go   8+
24. Bolting for Glory   10a
26. T2   11a s
27. Jules Verne   11a s
28. Lene's Dream   11b/c s
31. Guenese   11a

PROFILE OF THE
NAKED EDGE

SOUTH
BUTTRESS

UPPER
RAMP

26   27   28

CAVE PITCH

LOWER
RAMP

31

THE TRAMP

24

27   26

23

TALUS

RED GARDEN WALL – The Roof Routes

The Roof Routes are a series of difficult and technical routes that lie along the vertical red face between the Lower and Upper Ramps. The wall is characterized by a long, 90 degree, diagonal roof that forms the crux of several of the routes.

29. **Kloeberdanz 11a**
    Begin about 100 feet left of T2 near a large juniper tree. Climb a weird crack up to a large roof and crank over the lip.

30. **Kloeberdeath 13a s**
    Also known as Candallegro. Climb the first pitch of Kloeberdanz to the roof, then climb straight out the upside-down arete and up the wall (with poor protection) all the way to the bolt anchor on Guenese. Rack: #3 Friend and 6 QDs.

31. **Guenese 11a**
    This is one of the most popular of the Roof Routes because it is relatively easy and well-protected. Begin about 60 feet left of the juniper tree at a small flat spot in the talus. Rack: RPs and 6 QDs for first pitch; rack up to a #3 Friend to continue. The dihedral has been climbed straight up (11b/c s).

32. **Downpressor Man 12b**
    A good variation. Climb up and left from the first bolt on Guenese.

33. **Fire and Ice 12a**
    A popular testpiece a short way left of Guenese. Climb up and right past three bolts to an anchor beneath the roof. Lower off or climb the roof. A variation to the roof now goes up past two bolts to the left of the dihedral (12b/c).

34. **Psycho 12d**
    Classic. Begin at a short, right-angling ramp about 25 feet left of Fire and Ice. The roof is the crux.

35. **Wasabi 12c**
    Japanese hot radish. Begin with the first part of Psycho, then follow a line of bolts up and slightly left (11b). Lower off or climb the roof (12c). 7 bolts.

36. **Evangeline 11b/c A1**
    Classic. Begin at a short left-facing corner about 10 feet to the left of Psycho. Rack up to a #1.5 Friend.

37. **Temporary Like Achilles 10c s**
    Begin at a flake about 12 feet left of Evangeline. Climb either side of the flake, bearing in mind the obvious groundfall potential, then angle up and left to a line of bolts. Undertaker free climbs through the ten-foot roof at the top of the first pitch (13d).

38. **Hands in the Clouds 12a**
    Aid through the big roof on Temporary Like Achilles and belay at a bolt anchor. Then, follow a line of bolts up to the Psycho Slab. Rack: 6 QDs, stoppers, #1 and 3 Friend.

39. **Scary Canary 12b/c s**
    A very demanding route. Begin a short way up from the bottom of the Lower Ramp.

40. **The Wisdom 11d/12a s**
    This stupendous route has turned away many would-be ascents – not so much for its abundant difficulty, but for its lack of protection. Begin about 50 feet up the Lower Ramp, just above the end of a long slot. A variation called Saint Eve (12) climbs the original aid finish.

---

41. *Rosy Crucifixion* **10a**

Classic. From the top of the Lower Ramp, scramble back to the right behind a huge block, up a short corner, and down a ramp. Look for some pins and an obvious hand traverse out over empty space. Rack: up to a #2 Friend.

42. *Wild Kingdom* **12a**

This and Predator, its neighbor on the left, are long, exposed face pitches protected by bolts. Begin with Rosy Crucifixion. 165 feet. Rack: 8 QDs, #4 Rock, #7 Hex, #2.5 Friend.

43. *Predator* **12a**

Climb straight up through the roof from the first piton on Rosy Crucifixion. 165 feet. Rack: 9 QDs, #4 Rock (at roof), #7 Hex, #2.5 Friend.

44. *Ruper* **8**

Classic. Scramble up the Lower Ramp, climb through a notch to the north, and set the belay on a ledge eight feet higher. From the top of the third pitch, cross the Upper Ramp to a large cave, then hike down about 100 feet to a platform above a boulder. Three more vertical pitches lead to the T1-T2 Saddle. To descend, scramble east and south around the top of Tower Two and pick up the East Slab Descent Route. Rack up to a #4 Friend.

45. *Alice in Bucketland* **8+ s**

A steep and spectacular route. Begin from the Upper Ramp at the low end of the gigantic, arching roof (cave) to the left of Ruper. Rack up to a #3.5 Friend. From the sling belay at the top of the first pitch, a variation called Mad Hatter (8) works around the roof to the left, then straight up the wall.

46. *Super Spar* **10d**

Classic. This great combination, featuring a dramatic roof, usurps mileage from Super Slab, Grand Giraffe and Art's Spar. The latter two routes are not described.

47. *Super Slab* **10d**

A masterpiece. From the top of the Lower Ramp, scramble about 35 feet up a ledge to the west and belay beneath some fixed pins. The fourth pitch ascends the magnificent striped slab for which the route is named.

48. *Doub-Griffith* **11c s**

This demanding route takes a line not far to the left of Super Slab, but traverses back and forth from the belays on that route. An advent called Dubious Graffitti (11c/d) holds to the left and maintains a direct line up the southwest corner of the buttress. From the start to Super Slab, continue up the ledge for another 45 feet or so to where the wall bends around to the west. Begin with a thin, poorly-protected crack.

UPPER RAMP

LOWER RAMP

40

37

34

33

31

29

THE ROOF ROUTES
29. **Kloeberdanz   11a**
31. **Guenese   11a**
33. **Fire and Ice   12a**

34. **Psycho   12d**
37. **Temporary Like Achilles   10c s**
40. **The Wisdom   11d/12a s**

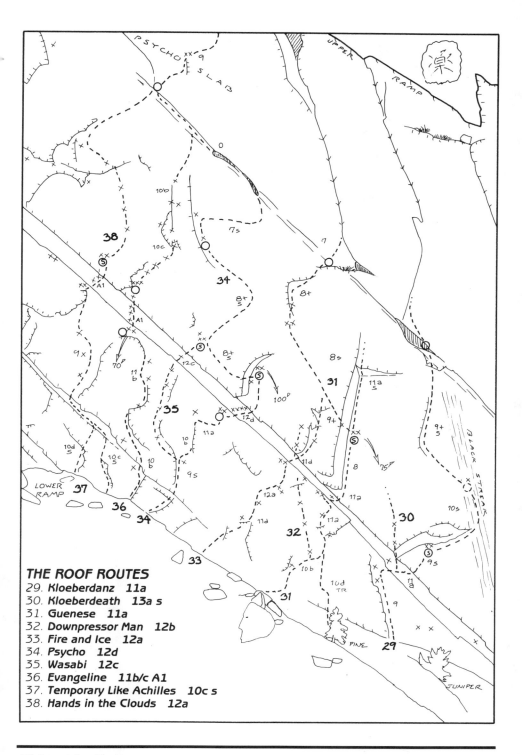

THE ROOF ROUTES
29. **Kloeberdanz   11a**
30. **Kloeberdeath   13a s**
31. **Guenese   11a**
32. **Downpressor Man   12b**
33. **Fire and Ice   12a**
34. **Psycho   12d**
35. **Wasabi   12c**
36. **Evangeline   11b/c A1**
37. **Temporary Like Achilles   10c s**
38. **Hands in the Clouds   12a**

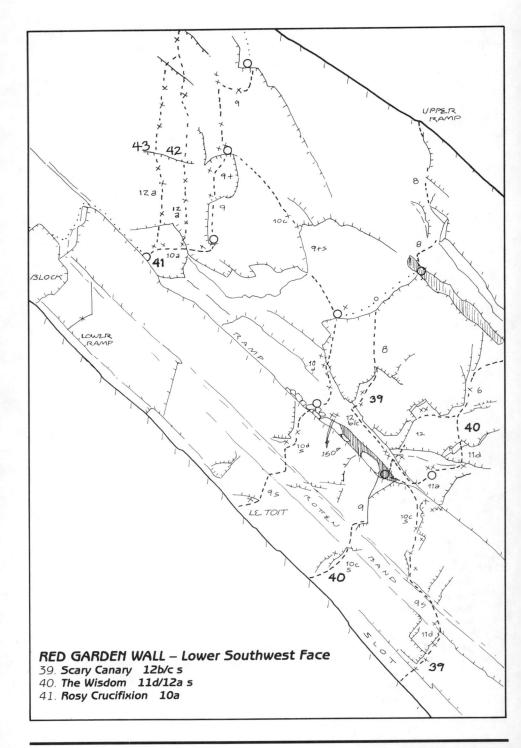

RED GARDEN WALL – Lower Southwest Face

39. **Scary Canary   12b/c s**
40. **The Wisdom   11d/12a s**
41. **Rosy Crucifixion   10a**

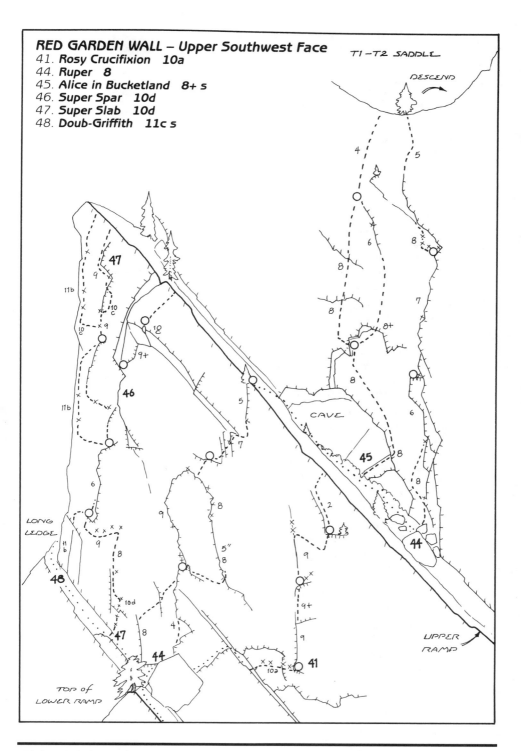

RED GARDEN WALL – Upper Southwest Face
41. **Rosy Crucifixion   10a**
44. **Ruper   8**
45. **Alice in Bucketland   8+ s**
46. **Super Spar   10d**
47. **Super Slab   10d**
48. **Doub-Griffith   11c s**

T1 –T2 SADDLE

DESCEND

CAVE

LONG LEDGE

TOP of LOWER RAMP

UPPER RAMP

RED GARDEN WALL – Lower West Face

The following routes begin about 400 feet up the West Face Trail below the top of the Lower Ramp.

49. **Suparete   11a/b**
    Just down and left from the juniper tree at the top of the Lower Ramp is a clean arete with four bolts.

50. **Mr. Natural   8+**
    Remember Zap Comix? Perhaps 150 feet beyond Suparete, a 60-foot hand crack shoots straight up to a ledge with a small tree.

To the left of the Mr. Natural find three, short, bolted slab climbs. See topo.

The following routes begin from a ledge that runs north from the top of the Lower Ramp and merges with the talus near the West Chimney. Access this ledge at a square cave some 800 feet up the West Face Trail, or farther to the north. It also may be reached by scrambling north from the top of the Lower Ramp (4). Descend from the routes via the Pigeon Crack rappel.

51. **Vertigo   11b**
    Classic. Begin at the south end of the ledge descrbed above, about 150 feet left from the start to Super Slab. Climb cracks and corners up through a spectacular roof.

52. **Mickey Mouse Nailup   9+ s**
    Begin behind a large tree about 30 feet left of Vertigo.

Tower One

This is the bullet-shaped summit west-northwest of Tower Two. Reach the following routes by hiking up the West Face Trail past a square cave to any of several weak points where one can scramble up onto a prominent ledge that leads south, all the way to the base of Vertigo. To descend, use the East Slab Descent Route or the Dirty Deed Rappel.

53. **Mellow Yellow   11d s**
    Classic. This awe-inspiring route ascends the southwest face of Tower One. Begin near a pine tree at the northwest extreme of the Upper Ramp. The A4 seam in the final roof has been free-climbed (12a) with the addition of some bolts.

54. **Idiot Wind   10c**
    From the top of the Upper ramp, climb thin cracks between Mellow Yellow and the Yellow Spur. Join the Yellow Spur at the top of the fifth pitch, move up and left past one or two bolts (left of the pin ladder), and belay on a ledge. Climb the smooth slab past a couple of bolts. No topo.

55. **The Yellow Spur   9   or 10b s**
    This route received the highest rating in the *Best of Boulder Climbs* survey. Begin up on a ledge about 75 feet north of the square cave. Open with some very steep and poorly-protected moves or take an easier start about 15 feet to the right. Seven pitches. Standard rack with 7 QDs.

56. **Icarus   6   or 8+ s**
    This airy line achieves magnificent position on the northwest side of Tower One and finishes with the last pitch of the Yellow Spur (6). Climb Rewritten or the Great Zot to a prominent ledge that cuts across the middle of the wall (the Red Ledge), then traverse about 70 feet south along the ledge and belay at the bottom of the Dirty Deed Chimney. Go another 15 feet or so to the south, out onto a rounded buttress, then climb up and right to gain a zigzag dihedral system. A spectacular variation traverses out to the right at a crack below the second belay and follows the arete to the summit (8+ s).

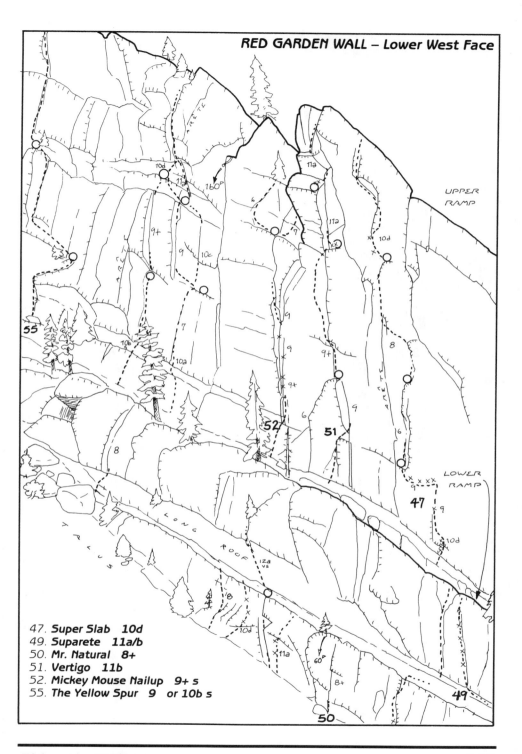

RED GARDEN WALL – Lower West Face

47. **Super Slab**   **10d**
49. **Suparete**   **11a/b**
50. **Mr. Natural**   **8+**
51. **Vertigo**   **11b**
52. **Mickey Mouse Nailup**   **9+ s**
55. **The Yellow Spur**   **9   or 10b s**

RED GARDEN WALL — West Face from the southwest

47. **Super Slab 10d**
50. **Mr. Natural 8+**
51. **Vertigo 11b**
53. **Mellow Yellow 11d s**

55. **The Yellow Spur 9   or 10b s**
63. **West Chimney 5 s**
68. **Grandmother's Challenge 10c**

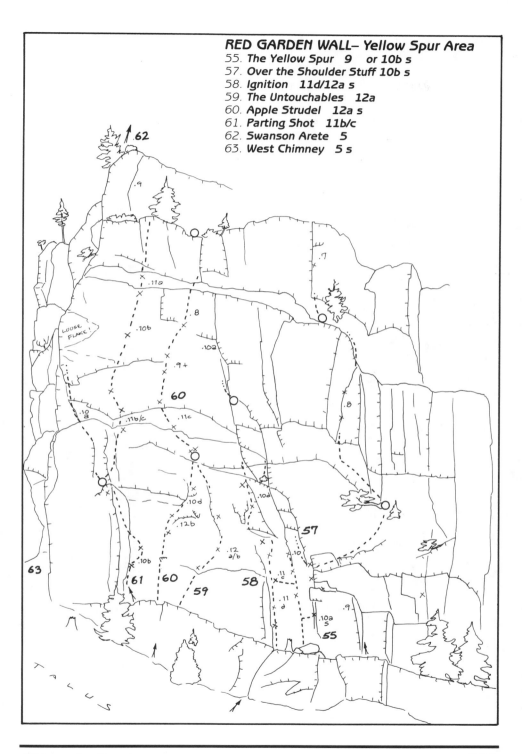

RED GARDEN WALL– Yellow Spur Area
55. The Yellow Spur   9   or 10b s
57. Over the Shoulder Stuff 10b s
58. Ignition   11d/12a s
59. The Untouchables   12a
60. Apple Strudel   12a s
61. Parting Shot   11b/c
62. Swanson Arete   5
63. West Chimney   5 s

RED GARDEN WALL — Lumpe Tower and Tower One from the west

51. **Vertigo   11b**
53. **Mellow Yellow   11d s**
55. **The Yellow Spur   9   or 10b s**

60. **Apple Strudel   12a s**
62. **Swanson Arete   5**
63. **West Chimney   5 s**

RED GARDEN WALL – Lumpe Tower

Lumpe Tower is the narrow buttress and summit immediately north of Tower One. It becomes distinct above the Red Ledge and is characterized by a clean, 300-foot west arete. The broad, steep face below the Red Ledge, continuous with Tower One, has several difficult routes. To descend from the summit, downclimb to the south about 60 feet to the col between Lumpe Tower and Tower One. Do the Dirty Deed rappel to the west or downclimb to the southeast via the East Slab Descent Route.

57. **Over the Shoulder Stuff 10b s**

Begin with the Yellow Spur, but work left from the lip of the roof on the first pitch. A variation continues straight up from the first moves of the Yellow Spur past three bolts (11b s).

58. **Ignition   11d/12a s**

This difficult route parallels Over the Shoulder on the left. Begin in a right-facing dihedral with bolts, or begin with the Yellow Spur and traverse left as shown in the topo. The latter option is called Transmission (11c).

59. **The Untouchables   12a**

Begin just right of Apple Strudel and climb up past three bolts to the belay on that route. This pitch is said to be much more difficult if you are short.

60. **Apple Strudel   12a s**

Classic. Two tough pitches. Begin about 50 right of the West Chimney.

61. **Parting Shot   11b/c**

A steep and excellent route. Begin a short way left of Apple Strudel – about 40 feet right of the West Chimney. A variation called Journey to Ithaca (10a s) goes left just before the roof.

62. **Swanson Arete   5**

Classic. This is one of the best easy climbs in Eldorado. Begin with Rewritten (6) but traverse up and right from the top of the first pitch to reach the Red Ledge. Start the climb from a high point up and right from the West Chimney rappel tree. As a variation, it is possible to climb part, or all, of the arete from the first belay to the tree near the summit (8 s). The regular route follows cracks on the right.

63. **West Chimney   5 s**

This is the deep cleft between Lumpe Tower and the Middle Buttress. The lower, 150-foot section sometimes is climbed by parties heading for Swanson Arete, but it is subject to rockfall and distinctly unaesthetic. It also is the last leg of the Dirty Deed rappel route. Perhaps, it is best to think of the West Chimney as a landmark rather than something to climb.

55. **The Yellow Spur   9   or 10b s**
56. **Icarus   6   or 8+ s**
62. **Swanson Arete   5**

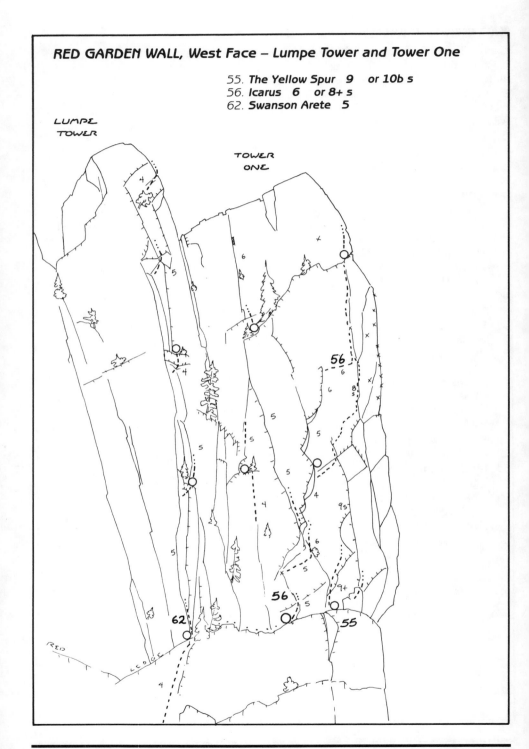

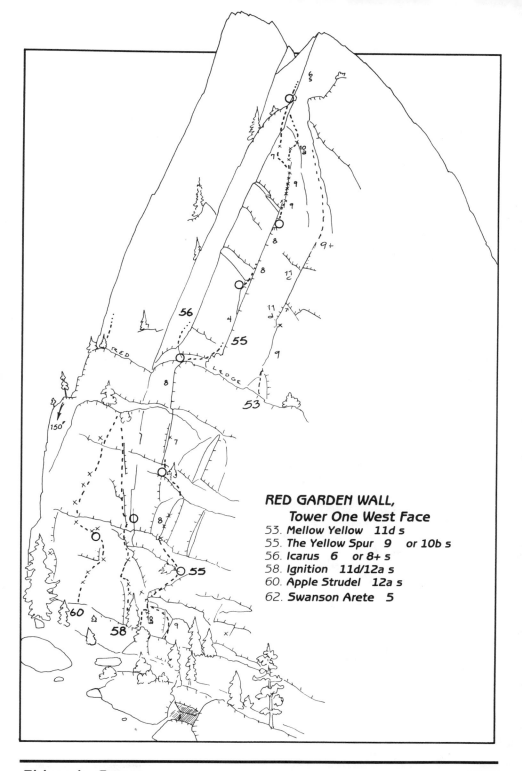

RED GARDEN WALL,
Tower One West Face

53. *Mellow Yellow* **11d s**
55. *The Yellow Spur* **9** or **10b s**
56. *Icarus* **6** or **8+ s**
58. *Ignition* **11d/12a s**
60. *Apple Strudel* **12a s**
62. *Swanson Arete* **5**

RED GARDEN WALL – Middle Buttress

This broad and rugged section of the west face is about 500 feet high and features several classic, multi-pitch routes. It extends northward from the West Chimney to a steep gully that separates it from the Hot Spur – the farthest north feature on the crag (not described). A greenish pinnacle called Rebuffat's Arete is the distinguishing feature of the upper wall. To descend from any route that reaches the ridge crest, scramble north along the east side of the crest to a notch beyond the Hot Spur, downclimb a gully to the west, then hike back along the base of the wall to the West Face Trail.

64. *The Great Zot* 8+
Begin just left of the West Chimney. Climb a shallow corner and crack up to a small cave, jam out through the top of the cave (8+), et cetera.

65. *Zot Face* 8+
This is the direct and logical finish to the Great Zot. Climb the first 40 feet or so of the fourth pitch of the Great Zot to a small stance, then angle up and right along a narrow ramp to a flake with a small tree, and continue.

66. *Rewritten* 7 or 8
This steep route features an exciting hand traverse and airy moves up the edge of a detached pinnacle called Rebuffat's Arete. Begin at the alcove at the base of the West Chimney as for the Great Zot, but work up to the left of that line.

The GC Arete is the overhanging spur around the corner from Rewritten. Its steep, flat southwest face features the Green Spur and the notorious Grandmother's Challenge (GC). The arete is fairly recognizable and thus serves as a useful refernce point in finding nearby routes.

67. *Green Spur* 9
Classic. Begin in a corner about 70 feet left of the West Chimney. Rappel after the first two pitches or continue up Rebuffat's Arete (above). One also may finish with the upper pitches of Green Slab Direct.

68. *Grandmother's Challenge* 10c
Classic. Begin about six feet left of the Green Spur, at the base of a wide crack that shoots up through a roof. Two pitches. Rack up to a #4 Friend.

69. *Darkness 'Til Dawn* 9+
In spite of its clandestine location and less-than-classic appearance, this actually is a very good pitch. Climb the crack in the deep inset behind the GC Arete. 140 feet. Rack up to a #4 Friend.

70. *Green Slab Direct* 9
The upper half of this route – above Red Ledge – is quite good and frequently is combined with Darkness 'til Dawn, Grandmother's Challenge, or the Green Spur. Find the less appealing, original start just left of Darkness 'til Dawn.

71. *Silver Raven* 11d
A very demanding route on good rock. Begin about 60 feet up the talus from the GC Arete in a rotten chimney. Crank up and left into a steep corner system. Two pitches. Rack up to a #4 Friend. One can avoid the loose second pitch by traversing left about eight feet and ascending the crux dihedral of the Grand Course (11a).

72. *The Grand Course* 10a or 11a
Classic. Belay from the ground or from the top of a pillar about 10 feet left of Silver Raven. Two pitches. Rack up to a #4 Friend.

73. **Paris Girl   13a s**

This was Christian's first "retro-route," but it turned out to be more controversial for its bolt placements than for having been bolted on rappel. There is serious groundfall potential in reaching the first bolt, and a long run-out after the last bolt. Follow a line of bolts up the narrow, 95-degree wall between the Grand Course and Disappearing Act. 7 bolts, 140 feet.

74. **Disappearing Act   11a**

Cracks and corners. Begin about 5 feet right of a chimney and about 25 left of the Grand Course. Two good pitches. Rack up to a #1.5 Friend plus a #4 Friend (at the beginning). A variation called Rabbits from Hats (10d) climbs straight up from the piton.

The exquisite second pitch of the Green Spur

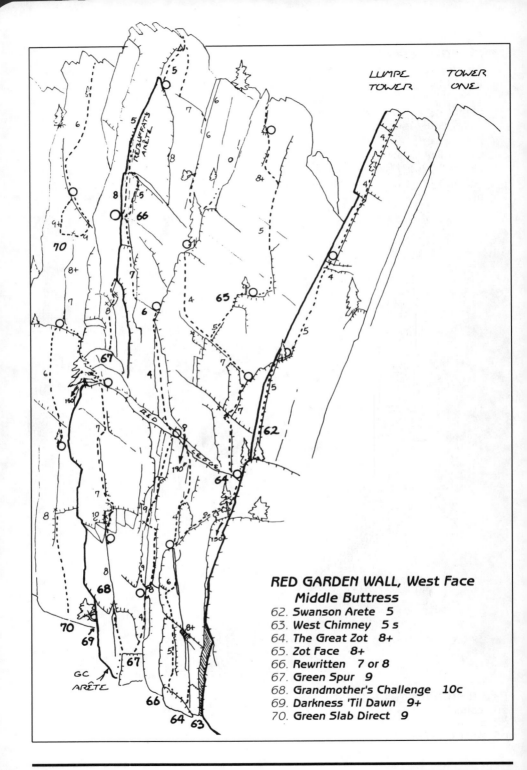

RED GARDEN WALL, West Face
Middle Buttress

62. Swanson Arete   5
63. West Chimney   5 s
64. The Great Zot   8+
65. Zot Face   8+
66. Rewritten   7 or 8
67. Green Spur   9
68. Grandmother's Challenge   10c
69. Darkness 'Til Dawn   9+
70. Green Slab Direct   9

RED GARDEN WALL – West Face

56. **Icarus** *6* or *8+ s*
62. **Swanson Arete** *5*
63. **West Chimney** *5 s*

66. **Rewritten** *7 or 8*
68. **Grandmother's Challenge** *10c*
70. **Green Slab Direct** *9*
74. **Disappearing Act** *11a*

Eldorado Canyon

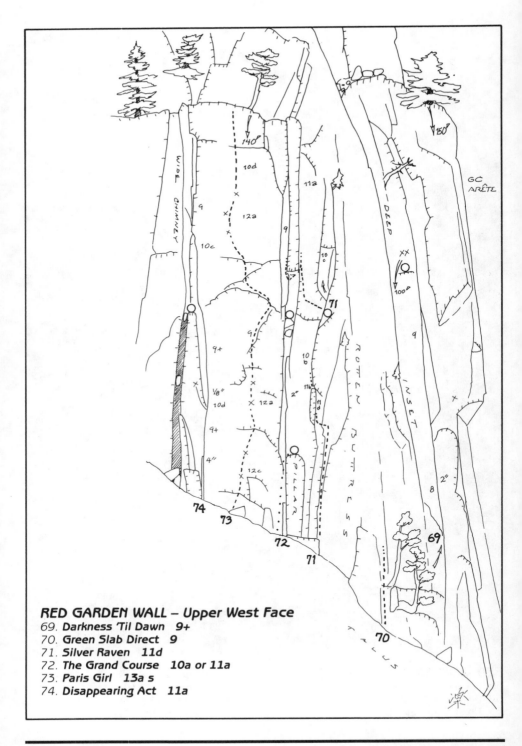

RED GARDEN WALL – Upper West Face
69. **Darkness 'Til Dawn** **9+**
70. **Green Slab Direct** **9**
71. **Silver Raven** **11d**
72. **The Grand Course** **10a or 11a**
73. **Paris Girl** **13a s**
74. **Disappearing Act** **11a**

The West Ridge and upper Red Garden Wall from the south

3. *The Unsaid   9*
7. *Long John Wall   8*
8. *Practice Wall   11a*

12. *Pony Express   11c*
14. *Xanadu   10a*

THE WEST RIDGE

The long and narrow West Ridge rises directly from South Boulder Creek about 400 feet west of Red Garden Wall. Its serrated spine then climbs some 2000 feet to the northwest where it terminates across a narrow gully from Rincon Wall. The ridge has more than 150 routes along the southwest face – many of exceptional quality – that range in length from 30-foot mini-routes to five-pitch classics like Long John Wall. Descents usually can be made back down the southwest side of the ridge via downclimb or rappel.

Approach. When South Boulder Creek is low or frozen over, it is easy enough to cross from the dirt road just above the Milton Boulder. Otherwise, it is best to hike the Streambank Trail and scramble over the bottom of the ridge to where the new West Ridge Trail begins. A ragged quarzite ridge intersects the West Ridge about 1200 feet above the creek. To reach routes above this point, it is easier to hike in via the Eldorado Canyon Trail and the Rincon Cut-Off. This upper section, set off by a steep gully on the south, is called the North Buttress and offers a wealth of great climbing.

THE WEST RIDGE – The Unsaid Area

Hike the West Ridge Trail to an area of right-facing dihedrals about 500 feet above the stream. All routes begin 25 feet up on a ledge.

1. **Cruisin' for Burgers   10c s**
   Begin beneath an obtuse, right-facing dihedral with a large, detached flake.
2. **Strawberry Shortcut   9+ s**
   This pitch takes the dihedral to the left of Cruisin'.
3. **The Unsaid   9**
   Classic – one of the most popular routes on the West Ridge. Begin at a leaning block beside a small tree. Climb a shallow right-facing dihedral past a couple of bulges.
4. **Washington Irving   6**
   Climb the right-facing dihedral 12 feet to the left of the Unsaid.
5. **Atom Smasher   12c**
   Begin from the tree at the top of Washington Irving and climb the right side of anarete past three bolts. Rack: several wires, #2 Friend, 6 QDs.

Long John Tower is the indistinct pinnacle about 150 feet left of the Unsaid Area.

6. **Incarnation   12d**
   This is a bolt route up the south face of Long John Tower. Begin on the east side of the crest. 90 feet. Rack up to a #2 Friend.
7. **Long John Wall   8**
   Classic. Begin about 60 feet left of the Unsaid at a right-facing corner. Five pitches. Rack up to a #4 Friend. Downclimb the east slabs or rappel west from trees.

WEST RIDGE – The Sidewall area

The Sidewall area is about 800 feet up from the stream and may be recognized by a series of clean, right-facing dihedrals above a bench. Scramble in from the left to get up on the bench.

8. **Practice Wall   11a**
   This combination route takes the first pitch of Practice Climb 101 and the second pitch of Sidewall (neither of which are described). From a pedestal at the left side of the bench, climb a steep right-facing dihedral to a sloping ledge, traverse down to the right and belay at two bolts. Stem up the beautiful corner.
9. **Warp Drive Overload   12b/c**
   Climb the arete left of the first pitch of Practice Wall. Two bolts, 60 feet.

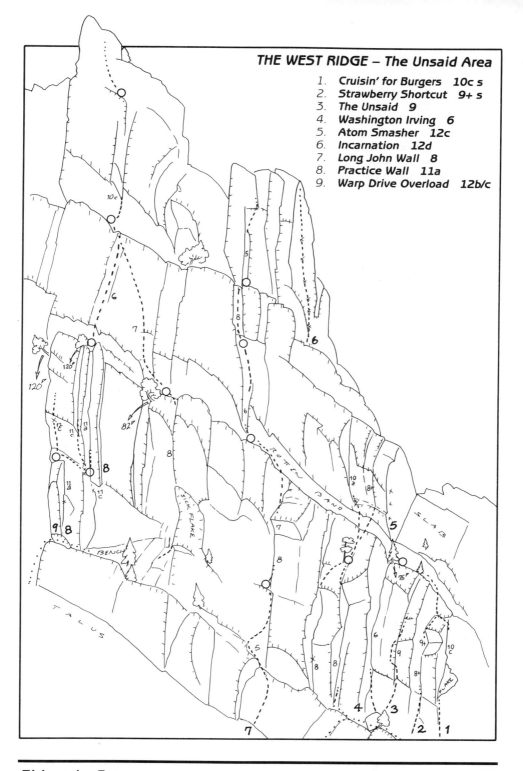

THE WEST RIDGE – The Unsaid Area

1. Cruisin' for Burgers   10c s
2. Strawberry Shortcut   9+ s
3. The Unsaid   9
4. Washington Irving   6
5. Atom Smasher   12c
6. Incarnation   12d
7. Long John Wall   8
8. Practice Wall   11a
9. Warp Drive Overload   12b/c

THE WEST RIDGE – Pony Express Area

The Pony Express area is about 1,000 feet above the creek and may be identified by a lone pine at the base of a very clean right-facing dihedral, 85 feet above the talus.

10. **Mesca-Line 7**
    Climb the crack that leads up to the right edge of the ledge with the lone pine.

11. **Iron Horse 11c**
    Superb. Begin from a ledge with a tree 15 feet off the ground. Climb the thin crack that leads straight up to the lone pine. Rack up to a #2 Friend.

12. **Pony Express 11c**
    Classic. Begin as for Iron Horse, but take the left crack. The second pitch takes the dihedral. Rack up to a #1.5 Friend.

13. **Iron Pony 11d**
    Climb Pony Express up to the bottom of the right-facing dihedral (about 20 feet below the belay ledge), move left on a flake, then climb straight up past 6 bolts.

THE WEST RIDGE – North Buttress

The North Buttress is the final feature of the West Ridge. It is most easily approached via the Eldorado Canyon Trail and the Rincon Cut-off. From Rincon Wall, hike south about 200 feet to reach the northwest corner of the buttress.

14. **Xanadu 10a**
    Classic. Begin at the south end of the face where the wall begins to curve around into a gully. Climb a buttress up into a long, left-facing dihedral with a thin crack. The right-facing dihedral on the left also can be climbed (9+).

15. **Friends in High Places 10a**
    Just right of Purple Haze, climb a crack up a slab, then a right-facing dihedral.

16. **Purple Haze 9**
    Hendrix Lives! Begin with the dihedral at the right side of the Chockstone block.

17. **Superstone 11b**
    Approach via the first pitch of Chockstone. Pull right above a small tree, clip a bolt and climb the steep right-facing dihedral.

18. **Chockstone 10a**
    Classic. Climb the finger and hand crack up the middle of the huge block near the center of the wall. Four pitches.

19. **Knight's Move 7**
    A good three-pitch route. Begin in the dihedral to the left of Chockstone.

20. **Jericho 11c s**
    An aesthetic and challenging route. Begin with the first 15 feet of Knight's Move, then break off to the left. The second pitch ascends a beautiful flared dihedral. Rack: standard, plus extra RPs and steelys.

21. **Muscular Dystrophy 11a**
    Hypertrophy is more like it. Begin at a clean, right-angling crack about 50 feet left of Chockstone. Two pitches.

22. **Laughing at the Moon 10c**
    A good face lift! Approach via the first pitch of Muscular Dystrophy, or via a clean dihedral to the left. bring a #4 Friend for the belay.

23. **Sirens of Titan 9**
    Begin around on the north side of the buttress. Climb a diagonal crack out to the arete on the right (9), then work straight up the narrow face.

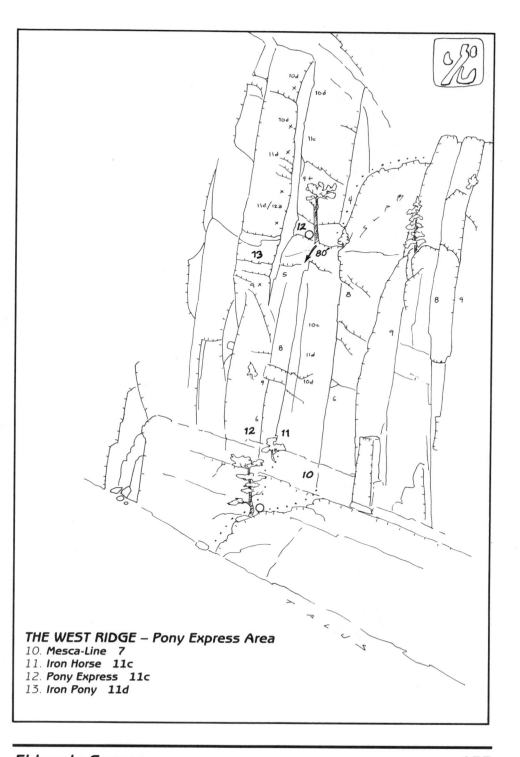

THE WEST RIDGE – Pony Express Area
10. *Mesca-Line* 7
11. *Iron Horse* 11c
12. *Pony Express* 11c
13. *Iron Pony* 11d

24. *Prince of Darkness* *11a*

From the beginning of the hand traverse on Sirens of Titan, climb straight up the wall past four bolts to the apex. Rack: a few stoppers, #2.5 Friend, and QDs.

THE WEST RIDGE – The North Buttress

14. **Xanadu** **10a**
18. **Chockstone** **10a**
20. **Jericho** **11c s**

21. **Muscular Dystrophy** **11a**
22. **Laughing at the Moon** **10c**
24. **Prince of Darkness** **11a**

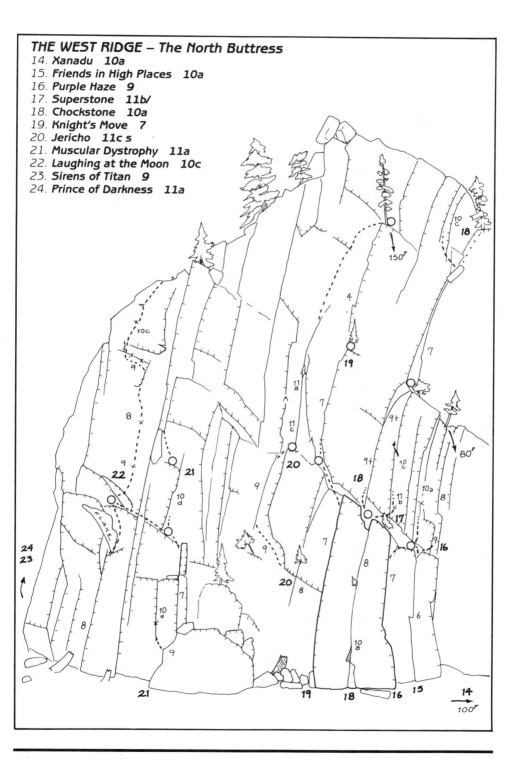

THE WEST RIDGE – The North Buttress

The crux of the Center Route, Rincon Wall photo: Greg Epperson

RINCON WALL

High above Eldorado Canyon and to the north of the West Ridge lies one of Boulder's premier crags. Superb climbing, scenic grandeur and relative tranquility await those willing to venture the 30-minute approach. Though one is less likely to climb here in solitude than ten years ago, it still is a breath of fresh air compared to the three-ring circus at the bottom of the canyon. The view across rolling green hills to the snowy peaks of the Great Divide cannot fail to lift the spirit and clear the mind.

Approach Rincon via the Eldorado Canyon Trail and the Rincon Cut- Off (see Trails, pages 84-85). To descend, rappel or downclimb as shown in the topos. Most of the longer routes finish on a broad ledge, high on the wall, that spans nearly the entire crag and can be hiked off to the north. The talus along the upper west side of the wall has been badly eroded by climbers, destroying plants and baring tree roots. Please hike next to the wall, and be gentle. Many beautiful trees, shrubs and wildflowers grow on the heights of Rincon and adjacent crags; they deserve your appreciation and respect.

RP	**Rincon Parking**	C	**Rincon Wall**
A	**The West Ridge**	D	**Cadillac Crag**
B	**The Potato Chip**		

RINCON WALL from the southwest
1. Point Break   11a
6. Rincon   11a s
11. Wendego   12a s/vs
15. Aerial Book   11a
17. Over the Hill   10b

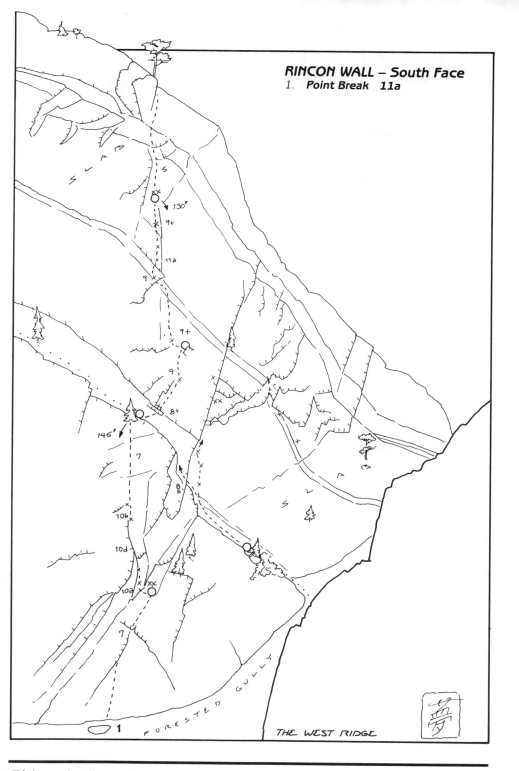

RINCON WALL – South Face
1. Point Break 11a

THE WEST RIDGE

RINCON WALL – Right-facing Dihedral Area

The southwest side of Rincon Wall is offset by a massive, 200-foot, right-facing dihedral that gives rise to the route Rincon. To the right is a steep, smooth slab with a series of vertical cracks. To the left is a dramatic wall with overhanging dihedrals and roofs.

1. **Point Break 11a**
    This steep and interesting route ascends the southwest shoulder of Rincon Wall just across the gully from the West Ridge. Climb a moderate slab to a bolt belay beside an overhanging, right-facing dihedral. Four pitches, the last two of which may be done as one. Rack up to a #2 Friend.

2. **Five-Eight Crack 8+**
    Climb the crack at the right of the slab to the rappel tree.

3. **Thunderbolt 11d s/vs**
    Climb discontinuous thin cracks to finish a few feet left of the rappel tree. Usually toproped.

4. **Five-Ten Crack 10a**
    Climb a shallow, right-facing dihedral with a small roof.

5. **Mind Over Matter 11c vs**
    Begin just left of Five-Ten Crack. Work up the face past the left end of an arching roof.

6. **Rincon 11a s**
    Classic. Begin with an exquisite finger crack, then climb the long dihedral at the right side of the face. Four pitches with direct finish. An old, bent piton protects the crux.

7. **Camouflage 12b/c**
    Follow a line of bolts between Rincon and Center Route. Rack: 9 QDs.

8. **Center Route 11a**
    Classic. Climb the steep flip-flop dihedral and crack about 20 feet left of Rincon. Rack up to a #4 Friend. The Olevsky Variation (10a) climbs the bulge and thin crack above the bolt belay of the first pitch; original finish goes right.

9. **Arete Bandits 10c/d s**
    This route parallels the second pitch of Center Route, a few feet to the left.

10. **Evictor 12c/ s**
    A very strenuous and difficult lead that is frequently toproped. Climb the beginning of Center Route to a downward-pointing flake, then angle up and left into a thin crack.

11. **Wendego 12a s/vs**
    Classic. The first pitch of this route is fantastic; however, the upward-driven pins that protect most of the difficult moves are old and rusting and have long outlived whatever margin of safety they might have provided. My recommendation is to replace the old pins with bolts. Begin beneath a massive, overhanging, left-facing dihedral that becomes vertical after about 45 feet. Rack up to a #1.5 Friend.

12. **Climb of the Century 11b/c s**
    Climb the overhanging dihedral to the left of Wendego.

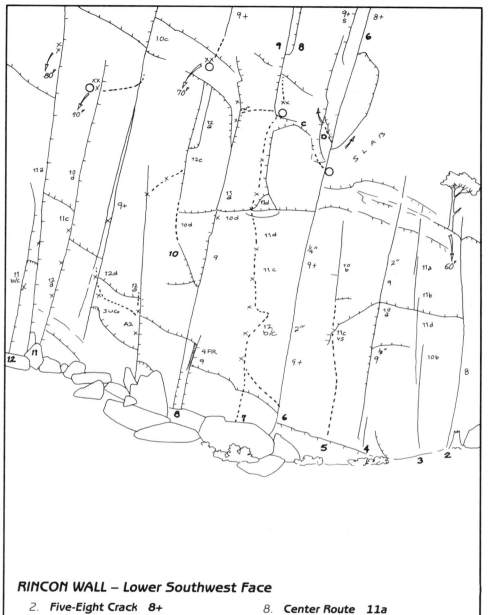

RINCON WALL – Lower Southwest Face

2. **Five-Eight Crack   8+**
3. **Thunderbolt   11d s/vs**
4. **Five-Ten Crack   10a**
5. **Mind Over Matter   11c vs**
6. **Rincon   11a s**
7. **Camouflage   12b/c**

8. **Center Route   11a**
9. **Arete Bandits   10c/d s**
10. **Evictor   12c s**
11. **Wendego   12a s/vs**
12. **Climb of the Century   11b/c s**

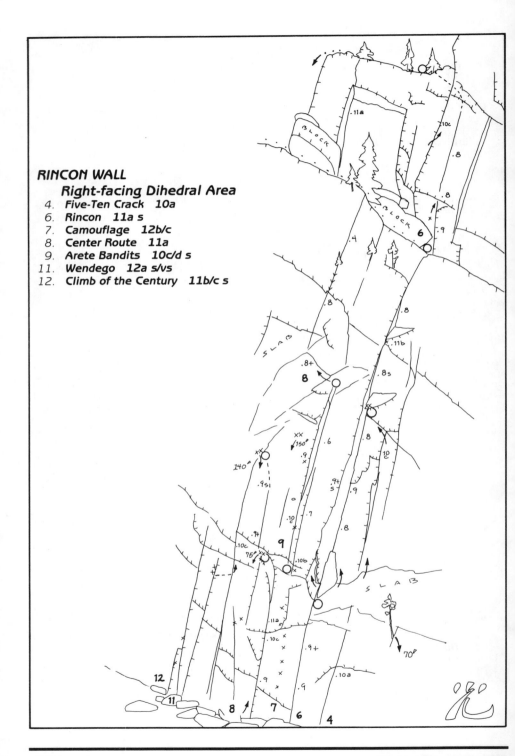

RINCON WALL
Right-facing Dihedral Area
4. **Five-Ten Crack   10a**
6. **Rincon   11a s**
7. **Camouflage   12b/c**
8. **Center Route   11a**
9. **Arete Bandits   10c/d s**
11. **Wendego   12a s/vs**
12. **Climb of the Century   11b/c s**

Climb of the Century

THE RINCON WALL – Left-facing Dihedral Area

The northwest side of Rincon Wall is characterized by a series of exceptionally well-formed dihedrals and aretes. All routes finish on a large ledge that can be descended to the northwest.

13. **Aerospace 11b**

    Classic– one of the finest face climbs in Eldorado. Begin just left of a detached flake at the bottom of the most southerly dihedral. Climb the corner for about 20 feet, then cut right to the arete (#9 Chouinard Stopper). Rappel after 160 feet or continue to the walk-off ledge via Aeronaut. Rack up to #2 Friend. A variation called Aerohead climbs the wall on the left after the first 90 feet.

14. **Aeronaut 11b**

    This route ascends the clean arete above the first long pitch of Aerospace. Traverse out left, crank over a roof, and work up the arete. Rack: RPs and 6 QDs.

15. **Aerial Book 11a**

    Classic. Climb the farthest right dihedral to a pin belay. Then, angle up and right to a peerless finger crack. Rappel 100 feet to the talus or climb up and right to join Aeronaut. Rack up to one inch.

16. **Aerial Bondage 12a vs**

    This difficult pitch is about 90 feet long and is protected by two bolts – a gracious gesture. From the bottom of Aerial Book, work up and left to the arete.

17. **Over the Hill 10b**

    Classic. Climb the second dihedral from the right, which may be identified by a narrow, detached flake about 10 feet up and a fixed pin a bit higher. Three great pitches. Be very careful of loose rock on ledges.

18. **Bachar Yer Aryan 11c/d**

    This route ascends the smooth face to the right of the third pitch of Over the Hill. Rack: RPs, HBs, and enough extra QDs to clip 8 bolts.

19. **Over and Out 8**

    An under-climbed route of good quality. Climb the dihedral left of Over the Hill, move left, up another dihedral, and finish with the last pitch of Over the Hill.

20. **Faulty Logic 10b**

    From the ledge at the base of Emerald City, move up and right to the arete, et cetera. Rack up to one inch.

21. **Emerald City 9**

    This excellent route climbs the third dihedral to the left of Aerospace. Finish as for Over and Out or scramble off to the north.

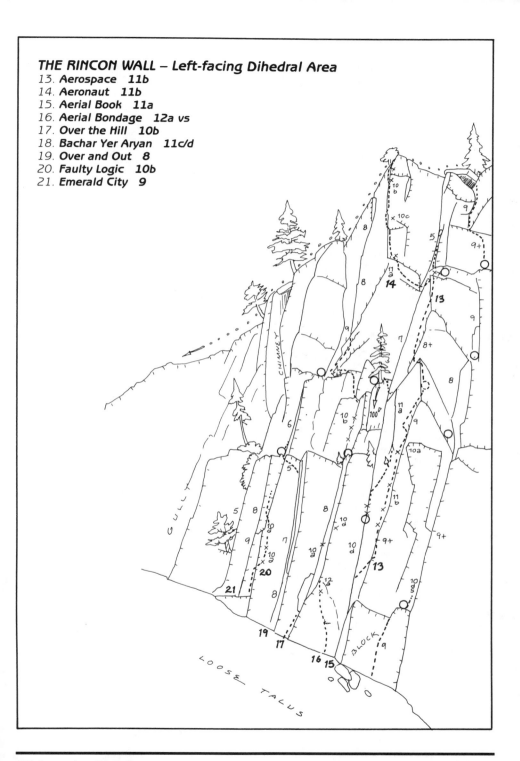

THE RINCON WALL – Left-facing Dihedral Area

CADILLAC CRAG

Anyone who has seen a 1960 Cadillac will understand the naming of this crag. About 100 yards northwest of Rincon Wall stand four dramatic fins of rock. The aretes are extremely narrow with steep, clean faces to either side. The second fin is the tallest, with its arete rising 170 feet above the talus.

Approach via the Eldorado Canyon Trail and the Rincon Cut-off. Shortly before reaching the talus field across from Rincon, branch off to the left and follow a footpath a little farther up the ridge to the north. After about 200 feet, enter a broad talus field and hike straight up the fall line. Pass between two tall dead trees, then contour north on a footpath to the base of the crag. Please avoid thrashing up and down the loose talus slope nearer the crag.

Fin One

The southernmost fin forms something of a free-standing tower and has a beautiful, flat-topped summit of solid rock. The routes begin from a tree 60 feet up the gully between the first and second fins. Rappel 160 feet down the north face or make two shorter rappels utilizing the tree in the gully.

1. **Ichiban Arete   10a**
   Climb the steep and beautiful face behind the tree to a bolt, then up and right to the arete. Rack: 3 QDs. Pronounced ee chee bhan: number one.

2. **Untitled   12a**
   This is an excellent route up the vertical north face. Begin as for Ichiban but go up and left from the first bolt. A variation called Flash Cadillac (11c) climbs a crack out right from the tree.

Fin Two

It is possible to down-climb from the summit over nasty, loose rock and descend to the north or south, but it is much easier to rappel 165 feet down the south face from two bolts. A short down-climb may be necessary.

3. **Land of Ra   11a**
   Ra is the ancient Egyptian god of the sun. Follow bolts and a finger crack up the middle of the south face. 5 bolts. Rack up to a #1.5 Friend plus a #3.5 or 4 Friend for a slot about 40 feet up.

4. **Highway of Diamonds   9+ s**
   Begin as for Land of Ra, but from the slot, move up and left to the arete. Rack up to a #3.5 or 4 Friend.

5. **Brand New Cadillac   11c s**
   Begin around on the north side. Climb the arete past two bolts, then work up and right to join Highway of Diamonds on the arete.

6. **The Black Face   12b**
   The north side of the second fin presents a clean, flat face of excellent rock. Climb the arete past two bolts, then move left to a line of bolts up the middle of the face. 10 bolts, 165 feet. Rack: RPs, a large TCU or mid-sized stopper, and 12 QDs.

Fin Three

To descend from the summit, hike off to the north on the walk-off ledge and follow a path back to the base of the fins. Or rappel down the north face.

7. **Star Gate   11c**

   A dramatic journey up the steep southwest face. Climb a steepening crack up to a belay niche, then crank left and follow a line of bolts to the top. 6 bolts. Rack up to a #3.5 Friend plus appropriate QDs.

8. **Moonlight Drive   10b**

   Nice climbing up the arete. Begin as for Star Gate but cut left to a flake, up and left to the arete, et cetera.

9. **Trail of Tears   12d**

   Begin this vertical foray around on the north face in a cave between the arete and a fallen block. Two cruxes. 13 bolts plus a two-bolt anchor at the top.

10. **V3   8 or 9**

    A good moderate route. Climb the steep dihedral between the third and fourth fins. Rack up to a #4 Friend. One also may climb a nice finger crack (9) just left of the middle section of the dihedral.

Fin Four

This is the farthest north of the four fins. To descend from the summit, follow a good ledge down to the north, then take a path back to the south. Or rappel from the two-bolt anchor atop Trail of Tears.

11. **Never Cry Wolf   11b**

    Climb the first 50 feet of V3, then move out left to a stance in a solution hole. Follow a line of bolts up the beautiful rock of the south face. Seven bolts, 165 feet. Rack: a few mid-range pieces for V3 and appropriate QDs.

12. **Gonzo   8**

    This popular crack climb is especially good combined with Deviant. Begin at the left side of the big block between the third and fourth fins. Two pitches. Rack up to a #4 Friend. Deviant is a steep finger crack that runs parallel and left of the regular second pitch (9+).

13. **Emission Control   10d**

    Climb straight up the arete or climb Gonzo to belay at a small tree. Move right past a bolt and climb the arete.

CADILLAC CRAG from the west

1. **Ichiban Arete   10a**
3. **Land of Ra   11a**
4. **Highway of Diamonds   9+ s**
6. **The Black Face   12b**
7. **Star Gate   11c**
8. **Moonlight Drive   10b**

10. **V3   8 or 9**
11. **Never Cry Wolf   11b**
12. **Gonzo   8**
13 **Emission Control   10d**

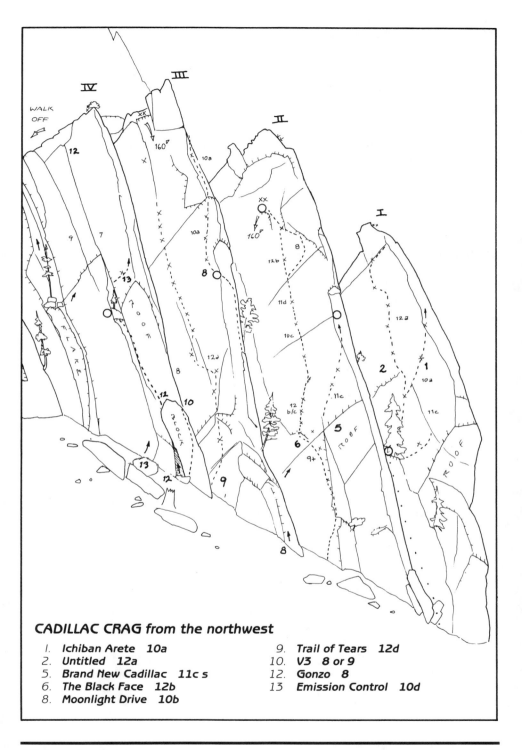

CADILLAC CRAG from the northwest

1.	Ichiban Arete 10a	9.	Trail of Tears 12d
2.	Untitled 12a	10.	V3 8 or 9
5.	Brand New Cadillac 11c s	12.	Gonzo 8
6.	The Black Face 12b	13	Emission Control 10d
8.	Moonlight Drive 10b		

THE BASTILLE

The Bastille is a landmark of Colorado climbing. This precipitous crag rises directly from the south side of the road about 200 feet from the main parking area. Its steep north and west faces offer a host of great routes, including the all-time classic, Bastille Crack. Though tiring, the long, 60-second approach is offset by dramatic views of Red Garden Wall and the surrounding canyon. Use extreme caution scrambling up steep talus to routes along the west side.

To descend from the top of the north face, cross a chasm to the south, scramble up into a diagonal slot, and follow a ledge southward to the Bastille Trail. Walk west a few paces. STAY CLOSE TO THE WALL and VERY CAREFULLY scramble down the steep, loose talus along the west side of the Bastille. Just before reaching the west buttress, pick up a short section of trail that angles out to the top of a large boulder and do the best you can to reach the road from there. This is a dangerous descent.

North face

The following routes begin from the road. Keep your rope out of the way of passing cars.

1. **March of Dimes   10c**
   This is a disjunct route with two good pitches and some mediocre rock in between. Perhaps it is best to think of it as a classy third pitch to Werk Supp and leave the rest. The first pitch and harder lines to either side can be toproped from a bolt anchor.

2. **Werk Supp   9+**
   A weird name, but a really good climb. Begin about 10 feet right of a small buttress at the left side of the north face. Climb a 150-foot crack and an overhanging, Yosemite-like slot. Rack up to a #4 Friend.

3. **Madame de Guillotine   12c**
   A beautiful stretch of face climbing between Werk Supp and the Bastille Crack. Begin with a left-angling finger crack (#0.5 Friend or equivalent), move up and right, and follow bolts to the belay atop the second pitch of the Bastille Crack. 165 feet.

4. **Northcutt Start   10d**
   Classic. Climb the steep, obtuse, left-facing dihedral just left of the Bastille Crack. Crank right at the ringed piton. Derek-Tissimo (12b TR) takes the arete just right of the Northcutt Start.

5. **Bastille Crack   7**
   The Classic. The crack is obvious from the road. Begin atop a pile of broken flakes. A word to the wise: from the flake on the first pitch, place pro in the crack BEFORE committing to the jams. Rack up to a #4 Friend. The first two pitches can be done as one 165-foot lead.

6. **Outer Space   10c s**
   Classic. Begin with the first two pitches of the Bastille Crack, then move up a ramp to the right, et cetera. The start to the second pitch is hard to protect.

7. **Hairstyles and Attitudes   12d**
   Aka Space Invaders II. This is a spectacular route up the steep face to the left of Outer Space. Begin about 12 feet down and left from the left-facing dihedral atop the first pitch of Outer Space. A sling belay is possible here from the first bolt, or belay from the ramp up and right from the top of the fourth pitch of the Bastille Crack. Follow a line of ring bolts to the top of the face. Rack: 10 QDs.

8. **Crossfire   11d**
Begin with the Bastille Crack and climb up to the left-facing flake. Continue straight up past a bolt (crux), over a narrow roof, up past another bolt, then right to the bolt anchor on X-M.

9. **Wide Country   11a s**
Classic. Begin atop the pile of broken flakes, just right of the Bastille Crack. Begin with unprotected moves (9) up into a shallow left-facing dihedral, et cetera. Four daring pitches. A variation called Times Square (12d/13a) goes straight up from the first bolt (now missing) on the first pitch. Two bolts.

10. **Direct North Face   11a s**
The ultimate tour of the Bastille. 1. Climb the first pitch of Wide Country to its common belay with X-M (11a s). 2. Climb the third pitch of X-M (10c s or 9+). 3. Climb straight up to merge with the first pitch of Outer Space (10a). 4. Climb the second pitch of Outer Space to the summit (10c).

11. **X-M   10c s/vs**
Classic. A note of caution: The rurp seam at the crux of the second pitch has suffered some deterioration over the years making the thin wire pro a bit more tenuous. Further, the belay anchor at the beginning of the pitch is utterly inadequate. Begin a few feet to the right of Wide Country. Five demanding pitches.

12. **Inner Space   11b/c s/vs**
This fantastic pitch goes out right from the third pitch of X-M. It also may be started from the second pitch of the Northwest Corner.

13. **Outer Face   10b/c s**
Begin from the diagonal ramp to the right of the last pitch of Outer Space and work up overhanging pockets.

14. **Northwest Corner   10c or 11a**
Classic. Begin below and a bit right of the X-M pinnacle. Undercling up and left across a slab, et cetera. Five pitches.

THE BASTILLE – North Face

2. *Werk Supp* 9+
5. *Bastille Crack* 7
6. *Outer Space* 10c s
11. *X-M* 10c s/vs

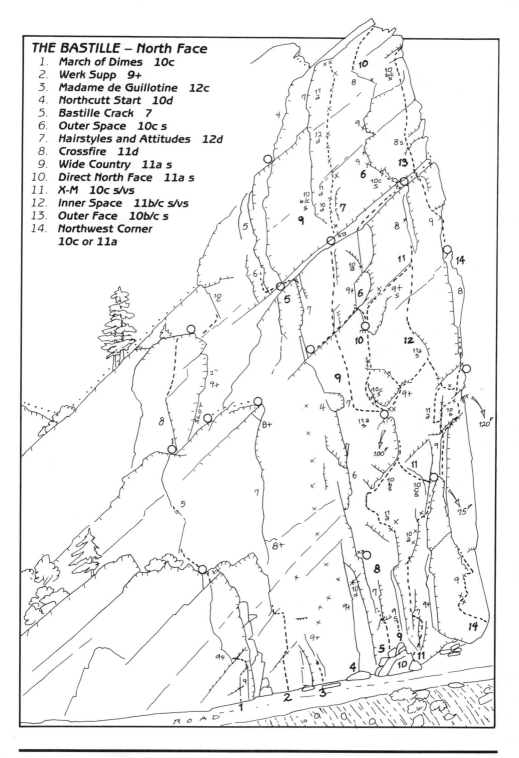

THE BASTILLE – North Face

1. March of Dimes   10c
2. Werk Supp   9+
3. Madame de Guillotine   12c
4. Northcutt Start   10d
5. Bastille Crack   7
6. Outer Space   10c s
7. Hairstyles and Attitudes   12d
8. Crossfire   11d
9. Wide Country   11a s
10. Direct North Face   11a s
11. X-M   10c s/vs
12. Inner Space   11b/c s/vs
13. Outer Face   10b/c s
14. Northwest Corner
    10c or 11a

THE BASTILLE – The West Buttress

The following routes begin from the unstable talus that rises steeply along the west side of the Bastille. Extreme caution should be taken while hiking or belaying in this area.

15. **Rain   10d s**
    Begin this steep and sustained route a very short way up and right of the Northwest Corner. One long pitch.

16. **West Buttress   9**
    Classic. Begin at a level area in the talus about 50 feet above the road, just below a huge boulder. Four pitches. A great variation is to climb straight up the thin crack above the initial fixed pins (10c).

17. **Hair City   9 s**
    Classic. Begin about 10 feet up and right from the West Buttress. Climb up into a shallow right-facing dihedral with a piton, mantel onto a narrow shelf, et cetera.

18. **West Face   10b s   or 11a**
    This ancient route ascends the right side of the west buttress, parallel to Hair City. Begin in the narrow, loose trough between the huge talus block and the main wall, but belay at the level area beneath the block. One also may climb the initial crack from the bottom (11a).

19. **Blind Faith   10a**
    The name of this route takes on a deeper dimension when one considers that it was established as a free solo. Begin about 40 feet up from the huge talus block beneath an obvious, continuous crack. Two interesting pitches. Rack up to a #4 Friend.

Summit Tower

The following routes begin above the walk-off ledge not far above the Bastille Trail.

20. **Neon Lights   11a**
    Work in from the left and climb the broad, rounded overhang via an obvious crack system (11a).

21. **Your Mother   12d**
    Spectacular air. Climb the broad overhang to the left of the second pitch of Neon Lights. Seven bolts to a two-bolt anchor. The crux is near the top.

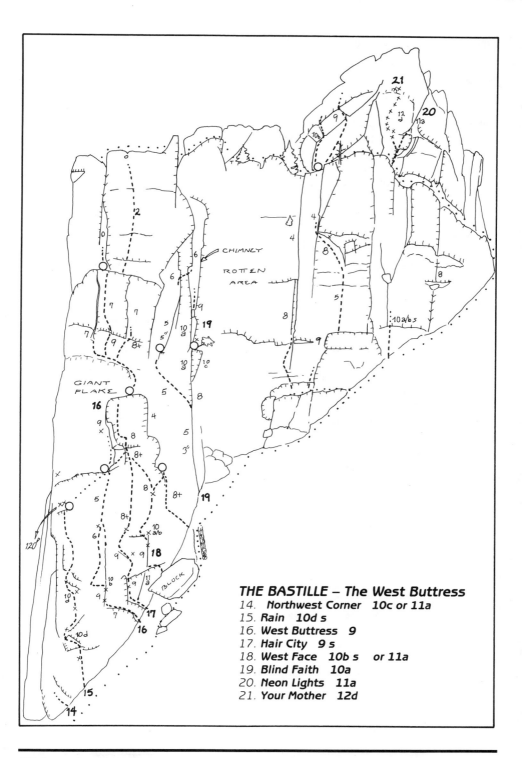

THE BASTILLE – The West Buttress

PEANUTS WALL

Peanuts Wall actually is two crags connected at a notch. These steep, north- and west-facing buttresses offer a number of excellent routes in an untrammeled, scenic environment. The walls are located above the Bastille Trail, about one quarter mile east of the trailhead. From the trail, head straight south up giant talus to the base of Lower Peanuts Wall, where a path winds along the base of the wall. To Reach Upper Peanuts Wall, continue up the path to the southwest. Please use the path to protect the fragile north-slope ecosystem of mosses and wildflowers.

To descend from the summit ridge of the Lower Wall, traverse south to the notch, then hike down to the northwest. To descend from the summit ridge of the Upper Wall, scramble northeast down a ramp to the notch, then down to the northwest, or downclimb to the top of Sunrider and rappel to a walk-off ledge.

Lower Peanuts Wall

1. **Blows Against the Empire   11b**
   Steep slab. Begin where the wall bends around to face northwest. Scramble up a ramp and right-facing dihedral to a large sloping ledge with a poor anchor. Rack up to a #1.5 Friend.

2. **Peanuts   9**
   Finger crack. Begin up and right from Blows. A variation called Scorpions (11c s), goes straight up.

3. **The Sacred and the Profane   12d s**
   This superb and extremely difficult route is seldom led due to the expanses between bolts, but it is easy to toprope. Climb the roof and blunt arete to the right of Peanuts. Rack: 3 QDs.

4. **Just Another Girl's Climb   12a**
   Difficult and sustained. This route ascends the face to the right of Sacred. 4 bolts.

5. **Your Basic Lieback   6**
   Climb the clean right-facing dihedral about 50 feet up the ramp from Girl's Climb.

The following two routes begin in a cleft, two ledges up.

6. **Wired   9+**
   Short but sweet. Climb a thin crack up and right across a slab.

7. **Forbidden Planet   11a**
   Superb face climbing. From the gully, climb around to the right side of the arete and up the steep face. Five bolts.

8. **Star Wars   8**
   Handcrack/lieback. Scramble up toward the right side of the crag and cut back left along the lower of two diagonal ledges. Two pitches. Choice of starts. Rack up to a #4 Friend.

9. **The Empire Strikes Back   11b vs**
   This is a cool pitch, but there is almost no protection other than a stray bolt near the top. Climb the obtuse dihedral to the right of the second pitch of Star Wars.

10. **Home Free   11b**
    Thin finger jams to steep face. Climb the large, obtuse, left- facing dihedral at the right side of the west face and the wall above past a couple of bolts. Two pitches.

Upper Peanuts Wall

1. **Gravity's Angel 11b**

   Begin below Sunrider at the bottom of the face, between a leaning block and a detatched flake. Climb up and right past five bolts. A #1.5 Friend is needed between the first and second bolts. Ace of Spades (10b/c) goes up and left from the second bolt through the apex of a roof. Include a #2.5 Friend and RPs.

2. **Advanced Rockcraft 12b s**

   This pitch ascends a beautiful, obtuse dihedral to the right of Gravity's Angel, but funky fixed pro has kept traffic to a minimum.

3. **Heavy Weather 9**

   A varied route that climbs all the way to the summit ridge in four pitches. Begin from a pedestal just right of Advanced Rockcraft.

To approach the following three routes, hike about 200 feet up the primitive path beneath the west face, then cut back to the north along a ledge. Avoid an eroded red gully that has been used as a "shortcut" to reach the ledge.

4. **Sunrider 11c**

   The sheer northwest arete of the Upper Wall catches the afternoon sun even in the dead of winter. Begin from a flat ledge at the base of the arete. Climb directly up past three bolts, then move to the RIGHT side of the arete at the fourth bolt. Stay right. Five bolts, 75 feet. A #4 or 5 RP may be used above the first bolt.

5. **Upstairs Dihedral 8**

   Climb the offwidth, fist and hand crack up the steep dihedral between Sunrider and the Cruise. Rack up to a #4 Friend.

6. **The Cruise 9**

   Climb the steep arete to the right of the Upstairs Dihedral. One bolt.

Eldorado Canyon   **157**

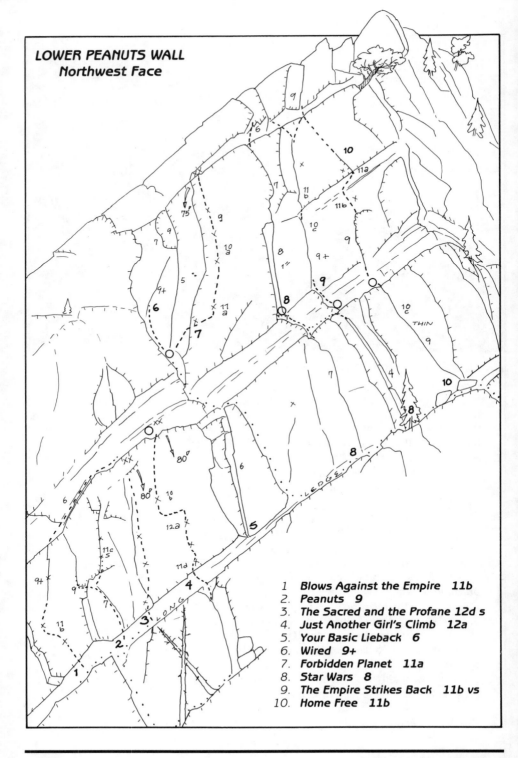

LOWER PEANUTS WALL
Northwest Face

1. **Blows Against the Empire   11b**
2. **Peanuts   9**
3. **The Sacred and the Profane 12d s**
4. **Just Another Girl's Climb   12a**
5. **Your Basic Lieback   6**
6. **Wired   9+**
7. **Forbidden Planet   11a**
8. **Star Wars   8**
9. **The Empire Strikes Back   11b vs**
10. **Home Free   11b**

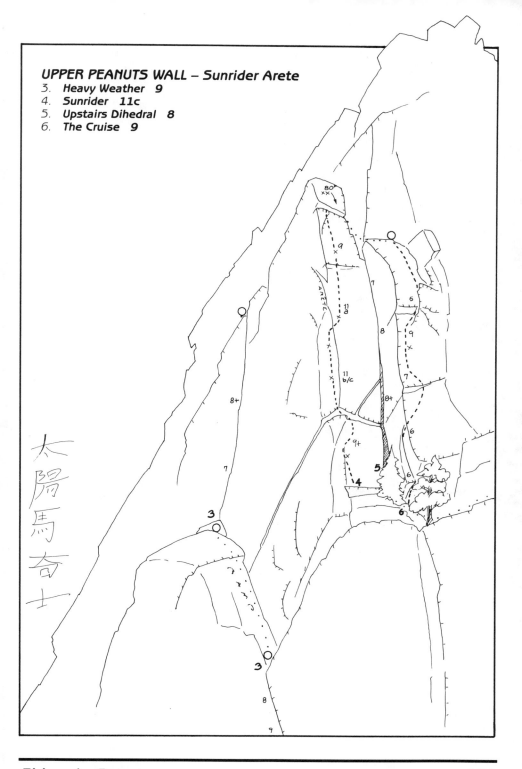

UPPER PEANUTS WALL – Sunrider Arete
3. *Heavy Weather* 9
4. *Sunrider* 11c
5. *Upstairs Dihedral* 8
6. *The Cruise* 9

NORTH TOWER

CENTRAL TOWER

SOUTH TOWER

R

7

29

22

16

14

9

4

3

MICKEY MOUSE WALL from the southwest

3. **The Offset   9 s**
4. **Asahi   10c**
7. **The Red Dihedral   12d s/vs**
8. **Boxcar Willie   11a s**
9. **Green Dihedral   7**
14. **Three Mousketeers   11c/d**
16. **Captain Beyond   10c**
22. **Perversion   9**
29. **Lifestream   11a**
R   **Rappel Route**

Mickey Mouse Wall

MICKEY MOUSE WALL IS ONE OF BOULDER'S best crags, but with its relatively long approach, it also is one of the least visited. It lies about an air-mile south of Eldorado Canyon, high on the northeast shoulder of Eldorado Mountain. From Boulder, it is recognized by the two huge knobs of rock at its summit that resemble a Mousketeer's beanie. The crag consists of North, Central and South Towers, which provide convenient divisions for identifying routes. Another notable feature is a long ledge that spans all three towers about one-third of the way up. The rock is the same, hard, conglomerate sandstone one finds in the Flatirons and Eldorado, but has a greater abundance of vertical cracks than its northern neighbors.

The main wall faces southwest, looking out across a secluded draw that forms a natural sanctuary, a place of serenity and rugged beauty. Stunted trees and bright lichens accent the steep faces that rise majestically above a glacier of giant talus. Eagles and hawks commonly are sighted. In contrast to this primitive setting, the Denver and Rio Grande Railroad nearly circumnavigates the mountain and runs through several long tunnels, one of which is blasted through the bottom of Mickey Mouse Wall. Alas, one does not escape the twentieth century.

Approach. Although one can hike to Mickey Mouse Wall from just west of the post office in Eldorado Springs (see map, page 80), the easiest option is via the railroad tracks that run beneath the wall. From Boulder, drive south on Highway 93 (Broadway), past Rocky Flats nuclear weapons plant, and turn west on Highway 72. After about one mile, turn north on the dirt road to Plainview, drive for a couple of miles and park just east of the railroad crossing. Walk about two miles north along the tracks and behold Mickey Mouse Wall after passing through the last of four tunnels. The drawback to this approach is that you may get railroad grease on your shoes, and the light at the end of the tunnel may not be sunshine.

Above the tracks, a nasty, eroded footpath climbs along the base of Micky Mouse Wall, which can be avoided by hiking up the large, stable talus field to the left. This greatly reduces human impact and affords good views of the routes as one proceeds. Other than the footpath, the area shows few signs of the usual human ravages.

Descent. The easiest descent from the top of the wall is to traverse as needed to the notch between the North and Central Towers and make four half-rope rappels to the big block at the bottom of Perversion. Traverse a ledge to the northwest to reach the talus. From the South Tower, it is easy to scramble around the back side of the Central Tower to reach this notch. From other points, it is possible to rappel from trees, and there are bolt anchors atop some of the newer routes.

South Tower

Shiva's Dance. At the bottom of the South Tower is a minor wall of exceptionally fine rock with several good, one-pitch climbs. The western part of the wall forms a buttress that is capped by a ledge. Rappel 75 feet from bolts at the west end of the ledge, or downclimb a ramp from the eastern side of the wall.

1. **Shiva's Dance   7**
   Climb a flake and short corner at the lower right side of the wall.

2. **Monks in the Gym   11c**
   The clean face with four bolts to the left of Shiva's Dance. Rack: mid-sized stoppers, QDs, and a #3 Friend for the belay.

3. **The Offset   9 s**
   Climb the very clean, offset, left-facing corner to the left of Monks. Rack: RPs, TCUs, and a #3 Friend for the belay.

4. **Asahi   10c**
   Steep arete and face to a finger crack. Begin about 75 feet left of the Offset, beneath a right-facing dihedral. Three bolts with the first on the right side of the arete. Two pitches. Traverse a ledge to the left to rappel from either pitch. Rack up to a #3.5 or 4 Friend.

5. **Perilous Journey   11d vs**
   A notorious no-pro classic. Begin about 15 feet left of Asahi. Climb the peerless face up and left past some pockets. The first 40 feet are the most difficult. 125 feet.

6. **Krystal Klyr   11b vs**
   Begin about 15 feet left from Perilous Journey, to the left of a blunt arete. Climb up and right around the roof/arete using a large, flat "krystal." Rack: a #2 and 2.5 Friend.

7. **The Red Dihedral   12d s/vs**
   This was a coveted aid climb for two decades, until it was climbed free during 1985. But no matter, aid or free, it gets you waaay out there. Begin in the large left-facing dihedral to the left of Krystal Klyr or climb any two pitches to reach the bottom of the enormous, overhanging corner for which the route is named. The state of the fixed pro is not known, but chances are it will be discouraging.

8. **Boxcar Willie   11a s**
   This compelling route ascends the wall just right of the Green Dihedral. Rappel 160 feet back to the ground, or make two shorter rappels. Rack: 5 QDs.

9. **Green Dihedral   7**
   Good routes in this grade are scarce. Begin with the first pitch of the Red Dihedral, then continue up the obvious left-arching corner. Two pitches. Rack up to a #4 Friend.

10. **Greenspace   12c**
    And you thought Joe Weider was the Master Blaster. Try this. Two pitches of difficult face climbing on beautiful rock. Climb the first 20 feet of the Red Dihedral, then move left into the line. Rack should include 7 QDs, a couple of mid-size TCUs, and a #3 Friend - QDs only for first pitch.

11. **Leap of Faith   12b s**
    The very thin crack to the left of Greenspace.
12. **Simian's Way   11a**
    The route features a finger crack and an overhanging offwidth slot. Four pitches. Begin to the right of a small tree, about 30 feet left of the Red Dihedral. Rack up to a #4 Friend. Dead Bird Crack (11a) avoids the flared offwidth section by climbing out to the right around a huge flake.
13. **Mighty Mouse   12b**
    This is the right of two good bolt routes about 80 feet left of the Red Dihedral. 70 feet. Rack: 8 QDs.
14. **Three Mousketeers   11c/d**
    Climb the clean face between Mighty Mouse and a left-facing dihedral. Beware of a loose block near the top of the pitch. Rack: 8 QDs.
15. **Culp's Fault   8**
    A good moderate route. Begin on a ledge 10 feet off the ground, between two left-facing corners. Two long pitches.

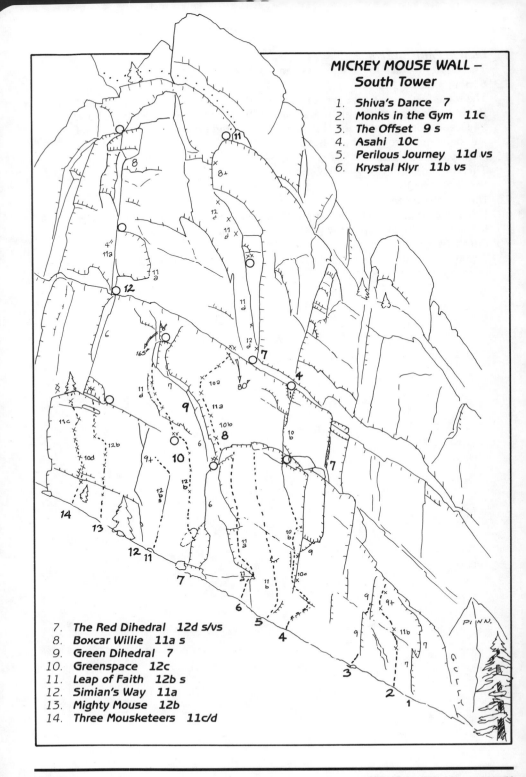

1. Shiva's Dance   7
2. Monks in the Gym   11c
3. The Offset   9 s
4. Asahi   10c
5. Perilous Journey   11d vs
6. Krystal Klyr   11b vs

7. The Red Dihedral   12d s/vs
8. Boxcar Willie   11a s
9. Green Dihedral   7
10. Greenspace   12c
11. Leap of Faith   12b s
12. Simian's Way   11a
13. Mighty Mouse   12b
14. Three Mousketeers   11c/d

Zen Effects, Mickey Mouse Wall

Central Tower

16. Captain Beyond   10c
This five-pitch classic offers an uncharacteristic amount of crack climbing for a Boulder route. Begin with a left-facing dihedral about eight feet left of Culp's Fault. Rack up to a #4 Friend.

17. Beginner's Mind   12a s/vs
Begin about 12 feet left of Captain Beyond and climb a beautiful, but poorly-protected thin crack. Rack up to one inch, with a #4 Crack 'n' Up for the crux.

18. Better Red Than Dead   12b s
Identify a line of bolts and cheater slings about 20 feet left of Beginner's Mind.

19. Rodent Lust   12b/c
Begin just right of Scorpius beneath a line of bolts. Climb up a smooth slab through the center of the initial traverse of Scorpius, then straight up the very steep face to join the arete at the top of the first pitch of Vergin'. Rack: 12 QDs.

20. Scorpius   11a vs
A very scary face climb. Begin up a ramp about 30 feet to the left of Better Red.

21. Vergin' on Perversion   11c
This is a good four-pitch climb that goes to the summit of the Central Tower. Begin with a thin crack about 30 feet right of the first pitch of Perversion. Rack up to 1 inch, plus 10 QDs.

22. Perversion   9
Classic. Traverse in from the left to gain the top of a huge boulder at the bottom of the Central Tower. Climb a right-facing dihedral to the Main Ledge, then follow the immense open book system up the middle of the face. Three or four pitches. Variations: A. Climb a clean, 90-degree, left-facing dihedral (9+) just right of the regular second pitch and merge with the main line after 70 feet. B. Vulcans Don't Lie (10b) climbs out through the middle of the big roof at the top of the route.

23. Zambezi   9+   or 11b s
Begin from the Main Ledge to the left of Perversion. The left variation to the first pitch is excellent. Three pitches.

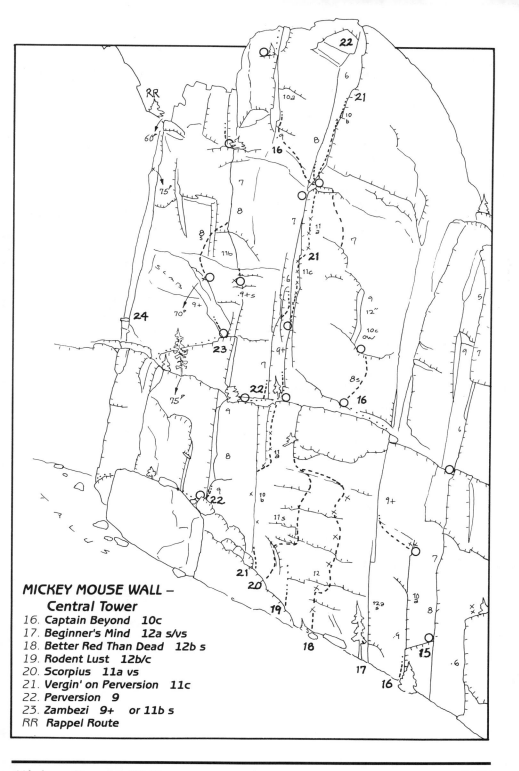

MICKEY MOUSE WALL –
Central Tower
16. **Captain Beyond   10c**
17. **Beginner's Mind   12a s/vs**
18. **Better Red Than Dead   12b s**
19. **Rodent Lust   12b/c**
20. **Scorpius   11a vs**
21. **Vergin' on Perversion   11c**
22. **Perversion   9**
23. **Zambezi   9+   or 11b s**
RR   **Rappel Route**

North Tower

The Shield is the distinct, bulging wall at the right side of the North Tower. One finds here both crack and face climbs of excellent quality.

24. *Parallel Journey* 9

Along the right margin of The Shield, locate two parallel cracks that are only about 6 feet apart. Begin with an easy, left-facing dihedral, then climb the crack on the right. Rack up to a #3.5 Friend.

25. *Don't Panic, It's Organic* 11a

The difficulty at the crux depends on how widely one can stem. Begin as for Parallel, but climb the crack on the left. Rack up to a #3.5 Friend.

26. *Fake Right, Go Left* 10c s

Only the beginning is difficult to protect. Climb straight up into the crack (10c s) or traverse in from the left (9 s). Rack up to a #4 Friend.

27. *Beagle's Ear* 11a

This great climb follows a crack straight up to the right side of an overhanging square block called the Beagle's Ear. Climb the first pitch of Lifestream, then scramble up and right to a ledge at the base of the crack. Rack up to a #4 Friend.

28. *Zen Effects* 12b

Sustained, difficult face climbing in spectacular position. From the top of the first pitch of Lifestream (10d), scramble up and right to a nice belay ledge just right from the bottom of the arete. Rack up to one inch for the first pitch; 10 QDs for the second.

29. *Lifestream* 11a

This route ascends the beautiful arete along the left edge of the Shield. Begin at the bottom of the wall, directly beneath the arete. Two pitches. Rack up to one inch and 9 QDs.

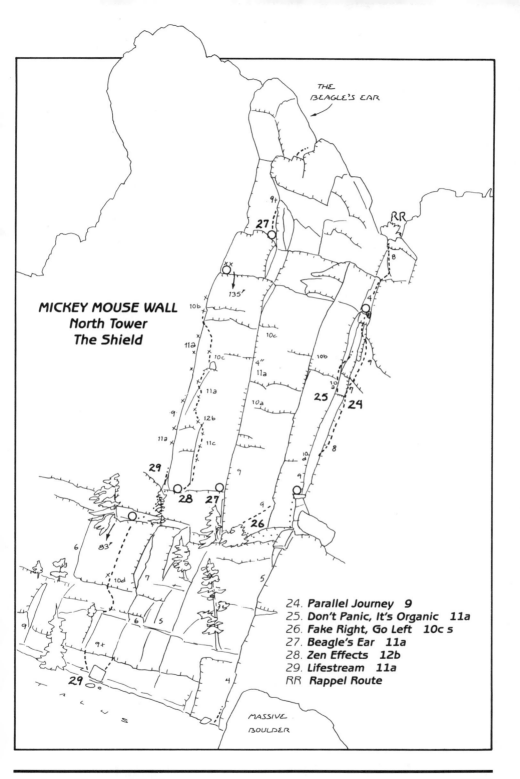

THE
BEAGLE'S EAR

RR

9+

27

XX

135'

MICKEY MOUSE WALL
North Tower
The Shield

10b

10c

11a

10c

4"
11a

10c

10b

11a

9

12b

11a

10a

25

24

11c

29

9

28   27

9

26

9

6   83'

10d

7

5

6   5

9

9+

29

4

24. *Parallel Journey   9*
25. *Don't Panic, It's Organic   11a*
26. *Fake Right, Go Left   10c s*
27. *Beagle's Ear   11a*
28. *Zen Effects   12b*
29. *Lifestream   11a*
RR *Rappel Route*

MASSIVE
BOULDER

Index